zen
and the
art of
screenwriting
2

zen and the art of screenwriting

MORE insights and interviews

William Froug

SILMAN-JAMES PRESS   LOS ANGELES

First Edition
10 9 8 7 6 5 4 3 2 1

Library of Congress Cataloging-in-Publication Data

Froug, William.
Zen and the art of screenwriting 2 : more insights and interviews /
Willian Froug. — 1st ed.   p. cm.
1. Motion picture authorship. 2. Screenwriters—Interviews.
I. Title
PN1996.F777 2000   808.2'3—dc21   00-061876

ISBN: 1-879505-56-8 (alk. paper)

Cover design by Wade Lageose

Printed and bound in the United States of America

Silman-James Press
1181 Angelo Drive
Beverly Hills, CA 90210

For Christine, Suzy, Nancy, Lisa, and Jonathan,
the loving and supportive Gibraltars of my life.

"If we are looking for something that can be 'defined' beyond all doubt, we desperately need someone to tell us that this kind of seeking is actually concealing the truth of Life from us."
— Karlfried Graf Durckheim, *Zen and Us*

Contents

Preface

In the five years since I completed writing my first *Zen and the Art of Screenwriting*, so many changes have occurred in the world of screenwriting that I decided it was time to expand on my popular earlier tome. Big things are happening to screenwriters, and they are happening fast.

The old-fashioned Syd Field paradigm is as out of date as the bunny hop. Screenwriters are using exciting new and complex structures to tell their film stories. (*Out of Sight* and *Get Shorty* are only two of many recent examples.) Today's writers are not only experimenting with radical screenplay structures, they also are bringing brand new attitudes about their place in American filmmaking. The top pros, young and old alike, are sick and tired of being treated as the peons of the film industry. They are demanding and earning new respect and recognition and have forced their own union to take them more seriously. In their own quiet way, our screenwriters are letting the American film industry know that they are "mad as hell and not going to take it anymore." They are, at last, beginning to feel their power. Their achievements today will directly affect every screenwriter who follows them, just as my generation directly affected today's writers.

The final decade of the 20th century also saw a film phenomenon that would have been unthinkable only a few years earlier, before the arrival of the World Wide Web. In a masterpiece of marketing and sales strategy, *The Blair Witch Project* was publicized as a film in which the actors improvised their dialogue (which is painfully obvious). Never has so much money been made from a movie that cost so little (allegedly $35,000, with box-office grosses of about one hundred million dollars). Brilliantly marketed through the Internet, this pseudo-documentary became the darling of the media. That the film is structured like a hulahoop—going around and around but getting nowhere—angered many. But the great majority loved it. It was the pet-rock movie of 1999. Subteen mob hysteria took over, calling to mind H. L. Mencken's dictum: "Nobody ever went broke underestimating the taste of the American public."

In spite of such occasional filmmaking flukes as *Blair Witch*, the most available and least expensive way to open the gates to Hollywood is still by writing a screenplay. But if you choose to become a screenwriter, I urge you to ignore what the studios say they want at any given moment. Studio management is always nervous. Attempting to second-guess the marketplace is a fool's game. So follow your own vision. If you are a writer, write. There are more wannabe producers and more independent production companies begging for material than there are good screenplays to shoot. Write a great one and you've got the film world by the tail. To paraphrase Phil Alden Robinson's *Field of Dreams*: Write it and they will come.

W.F.

Sarasota, FL, 5/2/2000

Acknowledgments

To my beloved Christine Michaels, sixteen years my best friend, lover, wife, and first and foremost editor. To the screenwriters who volunteered their time, again and again, and without whom all screens large and small would be blank, and to Bob Rosen, Dean of UCLA's nonpareil School of Theater Arts, Film, and Television, always a visionary whose single-minded dedication to film preservation and film history has set the world standard. Many thanks to Gwen Feldman and Jim Fox, who had a great idea ten years ago, started Silman-James Press on a shoestring, and nourished it like loving parents, making film studies available and affordable in print globally. Gratitude galore to my always superb editor, Jim Fox. Very special thanks to Dick Donner and Lauren Shuler-Donner, generous and marvelous people who welcomed me into their home with gracious hospitality, warmth, and encouragement, and to C.C. Labao, the majordomo of my Los Angeles adventures, a woman with charm, good humor, and sex appeal. Special thanks to the UCLA Emeriti/Retirement Services Center and its director, Eddie Murphy, and aide Eric Wang, and a very special thanks to Kathi Yamazaki, who cheerfully put all these hours of voices on pages. Hugs and kisses to the delightful Gretchen Thorson, my great teacher, whose almost weekly visits nimbly guided me through the maze of iMacdom. Thanks also to Jeff Caruso, future screenwriting star, for guiding me though the treacherous Los Angeles freeway madness, and to Joe Clara and Matt Hanna of Sound Advice. Much gratitude for continuous love and support from my beloved grandchildren: Hopi Hall, Ashley Hirano, and Andrew and Emily Froug, who help take the edge off aging. My cap is off to the Tennessee Screenwriting Association and the Austin Screenwriters League, great organizations that help countless screenwriters get started. Thanks to key grip Dicky Deats, a friend indeed when I was really in need. Thanks especially to Karen Pedersen of the Writers

Guild of America's James R. Webb Library. And a special remem-
brance to my friend and former student the late Jeffrey Boam, who
was a role model for screenwriters needing courage, commitment,
and the will to work. Jeffrey personified these qualities to the fullest.
A fine man, he will be missed.

A special acknowledgment to Frieda Lee Mock and Terry
Sanders and their American Film Foundation (www.american
filmfoundation.com), creators of the pioneering *Word Into Image* video
series and among the first filmmakers to bring recognition to the
primary role of screenwriters, for generously allowing me to quote
from their incomparable series.

Introduction

There has never been a better time to be a screenwriter. There are more markets available than there are movies to fill the screens. Remade and/or reworked movies have become a Hollywood staple, simply because there is not enough new material that excites producers.

As I write this, "Help Wanted" signs appear above the entrances to supermarkets, factories, and cafes all over America. There are more job openings than there are people willing to fill them. "Help Wanted" is also the plea of today's Hollywood producers, who are desperate for well-written screenplays. So even a beginning screenwriter with no previous credits or experience can get a million dollars for his or her first screenplay if it's exceptionally well written. As a beginner, nobody cares if you're white, black, pink, purple, male or female, gay or straight or both. And, believe it or not, even if you're over fifty (the single most serious crime in Hollywood), they'll forgive you if you've written a great screenplay. What's on the page is what's the rage.

Never before have stories been told by so many film and television writers (at latest count, the Writers Guild of America, west, has approximately 9,000 members, and its membership is climbing at the rate of about fifty new members a month). Yet we are only beginning to see the tip of a new, huge iceberg: As storytelling begins to invade the World Wide Web, producers are now shopping for writers of six-minute movies, three-minute movies—peanuts to feed the hungry audiences seated at computer keyboards. We cannot yet begin to imagine just how big the demand for Internet writers will be.

In spite of all the auteur-theory nonsense that still finds support among some film critics and many film school teachers who are still living in the '60s, Hollywood producers are reluctantly admitting that directors tell the stories *that writers have written first*. No writer, no screenplay; no screenplay, no movie. It's that simple.

Why else would the studios pay record-breaking prices in their bidding wars for screenplays? But a word of caution is in order. Even if your screenplay is brilliant, don't expect the motion picture establishment to welcome you with open arms—or even a genuine smile. The standard reply to a brilliant screenplay is, "Yes, it's very good but it needs work."

So why write? You write because you have to write, because you have an overpowering need to tell your stories. Or as Nicholas Kazan puts it, "I didn't choose to be a writer, it chose me."

"The universe is made of stories, not atoms."
— Muriel Rukeyser, *Written By*, January 2000

"It's all one story, really, the story of who we are and how we relate and how we get it wrong."
— Ron Bass, *The New Yorker*, January 24, 2000

"Whenever I am asked what kind of writing is the most lucrative, I have to say, a ransom note."
—Literary agent H. N. Swanson

Promises, Promises!

Hollywood is a land of ephemeral enthusiasms. It is as certain as smog that what agents, studio execs, stars, producers, directors, et al. fall madly in love with today will often hold only passing interest for them tomorrow. This is perhaps the most difficult lesson the screenwriter must learn.

I had dinner a couple of months ago with my former UCLA student and still good friend Eddie Baker [fictional name, true story]. Ed is an exceptionally intelligent man who has become a successful Hollywood screenwriting veteran, earning credits on two big-budget films. He understands the unpredictability and unreliability of the movers and shakers who work in the town.

Over coffee, Ed was waxing enthusiastic about a discussion of his latest screenplay that he'd had with Sam Osborne [fictional name], a world-renowned director. "Sam said he'd taken my screenplay with him on his recent flight to Miami and that, after reading page one, he couldn't stop until he'd read it all. 'It's perfect,' he told me. 'It'll be my next picture. And I'm not going to change a word; I'll shoot it the way it is. I'm tired of making conventional films. Your screenplay is new and exciting.' "

Because Eddie and I are friends, I gave him a hard time for swallowing that tired old Hollywood horseshit. But he was unfazed by my cautionary comments. He assured me that Osborne was on the level, and that everything would happen just as the director told him it would. Actually, I hadn't the slightest doubt that Osborne's enthusiasm for Eddie's script was genuine, as was his comment that it would be his next picture, because that was probably what he was feeling *at that moment.*

A couple of weeks after our dinner, Ed phoned to tell me that Osborne, after meeting with a major star, had decided not to direct Ed's screenplay, and that on rereading the script, Osborne realized that Eddie needed to change the protagonist's "arc." (For those of you not up on the latest Hollywood catchphrases, "arc" means just what you might guess it does: the development, change, or evolution of a story or a protagonist from the beginning of a screenplay to its end.) Then, uttering the most familiar and infamous cliché that screenwriters must endure, the director told Ed, "Don't get me wrong. I still love your script, but it needs work." Eddie, curiously enough, was not deterred. He was rushing ahead to do a major rewrite.

Why would my friend, a seasoned pro, fall for the oldest con in town? Because it's *not* a con. There's no doubt in my mind that Sam Osborne meant exactly what he said when he raved about the screenplay, and he also meant what he said when he advised Eddie that "it needs work." Hollywood thrives on short-term sincerity; it's the coin of the realm.

I tell you this cautionary tale to illustrate one of the most difficult ongoing problems for screenwriters in Hollywood. If you write a screenplay that is at all competent, I can promise you that somebody will come along in the course of your career and excitedly announce that it's terrific and ready to shoot. And you may well come away from this announcement feeling that fortune awaits you. Be warned: Enthusiasm, like the common cold, is infectious, especially in Hollywood. If you cannot accept this most basic and most disappointing aspect of moviemaking, you are in for a lot of pain and grief. And, worse yet, you can lead yourself down the dangerous path to depression.

The first lesson you must learn is that none of this craziness has to do with your screenplay. You, the creator of the characters and the story, are at the bottom of the food chain in a fast-moving environment where decisions are often whimsical and made on impulse. (Ironically, writers are both first and last in Hollywood's hierarchy.) That may be hard to accept, but it's the reality. Nobody is setting you up for a fall. Every hour of every day of the week, successful actors, directors, producers, and executives are talking about one screenplay ("property") or another, trying to decide whether to do this one or that one or neither one. These discussions sometimes go on for hours and sometimes for weeks, even years. Clint Eastwood decided to produce, direct, and star in *Unforgiven* seven years after he bought the screenplay.

The second lesson you must learn is that nothing said to you about the possible production of your screenplay is real. It doesn't matter who says it: It doesn't matter if that person is high up on the food chain, such as a studio head or an important star or an important director. Understand up front that it's all just horseshit. Walk away from it and get on with your work. As the Writers Guild of America warns you, nothing is real in the world of Hollywood until your agent officially tells you he or she has closed a deal. You must not write or rewrite a line until you receive that notification.

Warning: Promises in Hollywood are as toxic as the air you breathe. And, as my story illustrates, even seasoned pros can get caught up in ephemeral enthusiasm. We are so eager for our material to be appreciated, we are often left dumb and blind.

Rejection hurts, but whimsical promises taken seriously can often hurt even more. You are not likely to change how the industry conducts its business, but you can ease your own pain by working on yourself. How you handle life in Hollywood is not up to the system, it's entirely up to you.

Et Tu, Guru?

In recent years, scores of story-structure gurus have been touring the country with weekend seminars purported to be on the art and craft of screenwriting. But they only talk about the craft, the rudiments of which can be taught in a few hours. The study of art requires hours and hours of one-on-one work and, for most writers, is a slow, long-term process.

Craft, as most of these gurus see it, can be reduced to formulas: Go from Point A to Point B. Paint by the numbers. (But after sharing their formulas, they assure you that what they teach are not formulas. They only look, feel, and lay out on a blackboard like formulas.) These story-structure hucksters like to present screenwriting as a mathematical problem to be solved by placing particular structural goals on various arbitrary page numbers in your screenplay. (These page numbers will differ, depending on which guru you are listening to.) As Stephen Sondheim put it in his great musical *Gypsy*, "you gotta have a gimmick." One such gimmick (formula) is that there are 22 or 37 or 40 or 56 (you fill in the number) "steps" in a good screenplay, and that the inclusion of these steps will assure you a marketable script.

The problem with a formulaic approach to screenwriting is that there is no single formula, no one-size-fits-all. Good professional screenwriters wouldn't think of writing while wearing such a straitjacket. To accept that such a paradigm exists ignores the single most important aspect of screenwriting—the art of it. I can assure you that none of the screenwriters who wrote the classic screenplays that today's gurus analyze had any notion of "steps" or formulas in mind when they wrote. The creative process simply does not work that way.

How do the gurus discover their paradigms, gimmicks, and formulas? By analysis. Analyzing a screenplay may be a valuable research tool, but creative writing is something entirely different. Copying what some earlier screenwriter did by intuition is not the way to establish yourself as a screenwriter. Great screenwriters never follow a paradigm or count "steps."

Every script is (or should be) a new adventure, a new process of discovery. As you make your way through the wilderness, you should not be following a path cut by Lewis and Clark. Lewis and Clark did their job; now it's your turn.

Each generation comes along and builds on the work of those who came before. In so doing, each successive generation advances its art to a new level, finding new paths in its search for meaning and truth. Incidentally, it's a journey that you alone can take. It's an exploration into yourself, a search for your own personal muse. A big part of the excitement of working in the arts is that you get to go your own way, be a pathfinder. Where's the joy otherwise? Maybe you'll get lost, but maybe you'll find treasures. This is where the art is, the joy of being a writer, the source of great screenplays.

Story-structure gurus have managed to turn many a young writer away from what should be his or her prime focus—a personal vision of movie storytelling. One of the purposes of this book is to help return the focus to where it belongs: the *art* of screenwriting.

Enter Mr. Lee

Everybody seems to want a shortcut to screenwriting success. For those of you looking for a formula, here is the best one I've read. It comes from a most unexpected source.

> "Research your own experience for the truth. Absorb what is useful. . . .
> Add what is specifically your own. . . . The creating individual . . . is more
> important than any style or system."
> —Bruce Lee, martial arts master

Search your history and, more importantly, search the history of your feelings. When you recall your own pains and the events that created them, you will find your drama and your comedy. It will not come easily, because all of us tend to bury pain, to forget it. But pain can be your personal gold mine.

Most great writers work from their deepest passions, which are often the passions of pain. They transpose these into their characters, which is what gives us a sense of their reality, their believability. As Scott Frank puts it, characters are written "from the inside out," not the other way around (which, by the way, tells you why all formulas are phony).

Adventuresome writers also know that stories, like characters, create their own structure.

"A fleeting moment goes by, and I say, "Hey, that would make an idea for a play. That would make an idea for a movie." Sometimes it's as simple as just sitting down and thinking, without the slightest idea of what it is that I'm gonna write about. And I could just sit in this chair for hours with a pad and a pencil and say, "What is it you want to write about?" . . . Quite often it comes out of what it is that I am going through at the moment. Sometimes it precedes what I am about to go through. I think the best ideas come together at the same time. In other words, the most interesting characters plus a very interesting conflict. If I just have one without the other, then I'm not sure where the thing is going."

—Neil Simon, from *Word Into Image*
(courtesy of American Film Foundation)

One Singularly Superb Writer

An Interview with

Aaron Sorkin

"Anytime you have a story about an ordinary person in an extraordinary situation, you are in business."

— Aaron Sorkin

There is something quite special about Aaron Sorkin's screenplays: His stories are carefully crafted. His dialogue is surgically sharp. He wastes no time getting to the key moments. His characters are direct and driven by their needs. As it turns out, so is Mr. Sorkin.

I was forewarned by his fellow screenwriters that he is truly " brilliant." But since hyperbole is coin of the realm in Hollywood, I had few expectations as I walked around the massive sound stages of the Disney Studios lot one foggy Friday morning, heading to Sorkin's office. There is a strong sense of tidiness about this Burbank studio that one does not encounter with the older motion picture lots. The Disney studio itself is like a giant cartoon of a Hollywood moviemaking machine—everything clean, simple, and sanitary, painted a drab, no-nonsense gray. It looks like it belongs near Park Place on a Monopoly board.

In his office, above one of the sound stages, I found Sorkin seated in a chair beside his desk, patiently awaiting our interview. He is a handsome young man, neatly dressed and clean-cut. He could easily pass for a successful Wall Street stockbroker. However, nothing about this writer's cool presence prepared me for the laughter that flowed throughout our brief conversation. Sorkin is the type of writer and storyteller who can get laughs without jokes. The target of his humor is often himself; he seems comfortable in his own skin. And he obviously enjoys being a player in the absurdist comedy we call Hollywood. The life of the Hollywood screenwriter has never been more delightfully told.

FROUG: Your play *A Few Good Men* was a big hit on Broadway. I presume it has a two-act structure, right?

SORKIN: As a play, it was a two-act play, yes.

FROUG: When you wrote the screenplay, how did you adjust the play to the conventional three-act movie structure?

SORKIN: That was the most difficult job, taking it from play to movie. When I wrote the screenplay for *A Few Good Men*, not only had I never written a screenplay before, I had never read a screenplay before. I didn't know much about movies at all. I had been a student of plays. Friends of mine who had grown up with movies could tell you who was the set decorator and assistant director on all Alfred Hitchcock's movies. They had gone to lots of movies as students, but I had gone to plays. I didn't know anything about movies, so I read as many screenplays as I could. I started to pay attention to movies, and I tried to figure out how to kind of crowbar this story into a three-act structure, which I was told movies have to be. So I fiddled around with the placement of some emotional climaxes in the story and then managed to turn it into three acts.

FROUG: Did you look for certain developments—perhaps some sort of a major event on page twenty-something and a climax on, let's say, page eighty-something?

SORKIN: Yes, in fact, I did, although I rarely work that scientifically. For instance, the act-one curtain in the play is just after he pleads not guilty on behalf of his clients, and he turns around and says, "This is what a courtroom looks like." That's the play's act-one

"When I wrote the screenplay for A Few Good Men, *not only had I never written a screenplay before, I had never read a screenplay before."*

curtain line, and certainly an emotional climax. I moved it up just a little bit in the film, and I found a second one that could come some thirty or forty pages later and sort of faked my way through a three-act structure.

FROUG: You did a hell of a job of faking. Did you do many rewrites?

SORKIN: Of the film? Many. First of all, I should tell you that I did many rewrites of the play first. It was ten years ago now that I wrote it. I was a very new writer, and this was really on-the-job training, so I would write draft after draft after draft. Once we went into rehearsals, I would rewrite it every day. Once we began out-of-town tryouts, I rewrote it a lot more. I would rewrite every day, even during previews on Broadway, and continue rewriting during the run. I really was looking forward to the opportunity to do the screenplay because it gave me a chance to rewrite it once again after having gotten to see it for a year and a half on Broadway. Once I did the original draft of that screenplay, which was very long, I did another draft, made some trims, and finally got it into a shooting script.

FROUG: After it was cast, and Jack Nicholson was onboard, were there more rewrites?

SORKIN: They were tiny. I remember that sometime after Nicholson was cast, the script was still running long and I needed to just trim some pages off. I made a cut in Jack's courtroom speech, and Rob Reiner read it and said, "My God! You can touch anything you want in the script, but not this. This speech is half the reason we're paying this guy five million dollars."

FROUG: Were you happy with the movie?

SORKIN: Very happy.

FROUG: Then you went from that to a comedy, *The American President*. Tell me about that experience.

SORKIN: No. I went from that to a thriller called *Malice*.

FROUG: *Malice* is like two movies. There's a movie about a janitor who is a serial rapist and killer, strangling girls on campus, and then there's a movie about a doctor and a young woman who are working a scam to bilk a malpractice insurance company. It's an odd screenplay with two different stories going on at the same time. How come?

SORKIN: Today is your lucky day. You are actually seeing the two authors of those two movies back to back. Scott Frank wrote the movie about the janitor. I wrote the other one about the doctor-patient scam.

FROUG: How did that happen?

SORKIN: Before my *Few Good Men* screenplay, when all I had was the play of *A Few Good Men*, which was just about to start rehearsal in New York, Castle Rock bought a pitch, an idea, from a writer named Jonas McCord. This writer had heard a rumor that a Beverly Hills surgeon and a young woman had conspired together to defraud an insurance company with a malpractice suit. The nature of the fraud was that he was to operate on her, screwing up the operation in a kind of non-fatal, non-painful way, but in a manner that would give her grounds to sue him for a lot of money, and they'd split the loot. Castle Rock hired Jonas McCord to write it. McCord was unable to write it. In the meantime, Castle Rock had worked very closely with writer William Goldman. They wanted Bill Goldman to write it, but he did not have the time. So he said, "I'd like you to go out and identify a new young writer who I can take under my wing and mentor. I'll work with him on the story and watch him develop the screenplay." Castle Rock had read my play *A Few Good Men* and decided I was that guy.

So I came in and wrote the first two drafts of the script, a psychological thriller about this brilliant young doctor—very charismatic, very charming—in a sleepy New England college town who gets together with the wife of a young professor and does this. Her reason is the loot. His reason is slightly different. He understands that he has a psychological problem, a mental problem, and that the scalpel should be taken out of his hands, but he needs to be able to support himself for the rest of his life.

"... when I was done with A Few Good Men, *I was brought back to* Malice. *But by that time there was the story of a serial-murdering janitor."*

By the time I turned in the second draft of *Malice*, Castle Rock had acquired film rights to *A Few Good Men*, which Rob Reiner badly wanted to direct. And he wanted to start right away—tomorrow; he did not want to wait for me to finish writing the third draft of *Malice*. So Castle Rock made a corporate decision: They took me off of *Malice* and had me begin writing the *Few Good Men* screenplay right away. They brought in Scott Frank to finish off the process of writing *Malice*.

While I was writing the *Few Good Men* screenplay, they signed Harold Becker to direct *Malice*, and Nicole Kidman to star in it. For whatever reason, Harold was not very happy with Scott's drafts. So when I was done with *A Few Good Men*, I was brought back to *Malice*. But by that time there was the story of a serial-murdering janitor. It was a much different movie. It wasn't my movie anymore; I was a writer for hire, a hired gun, on my own movie. My job was really to write the doctor so we could get Alec Baldwin. Those were my marching orders, and I did as I was told. That is why the credits for *Malice* read story by me and Jonas McCord, screenplay by me and Scott Frank.

FROUG: You and Scott Frank never actually collaborated?

SORKIN: No. We never were in the same room at the same time.

FROUG: Do you know each other?

SORKIN: We do know each other. I am very fond of Scott.

FROUG: So there are no hard feelings?

SORKIN: I don't think so. Certainly not on my end.

FROUG: So the movie is two stories pieced together by different writers with different concepts of what the story should be about?

SORKIN: It might even be more than two movies pieced together. And the movie, in the end, didn't work. I am sad about that.

FROUG: Is *An American President* an outgrowth of *A Few Good Men*?

SORKIN: Yes, it is in this way: After *A Few Good Men*, Rob Reiner decided that he wanted us to do another movie together, another Washington-based movie with Tom Cruise, and Tom Cruise said he wanted to do another movie with us as well.

Here's how these things happen; here's the story: We had no idea what this movie was going to be about. It was simply to be directed by Rob Reiner, written by me, starring Tom Cruise. The three of us were going to have lunch one day when I got a phone call early that morning from Rob Reiner, saying, "Listen, I just got a phone call from Warren Beatty. He hears that the three of us are going to be doing kind of a political, Washington movie and he would like to be in it. Is there a part for Warren Beatty?" And I said. "Probably. Since I haven't started writing, there's a part for whomever. Besides, having lunch with Warren Beatty would be fun, and we should do that." So the four of us . . .

FROUG: Now you have Beatty, Cruise, Reiner, and Sorkin at lunch talking about this movie that doesn't exist, not even a story so far?

SORKIN: Yeah. The four of us had lunch that afternoon on Maple Drive [Beverly Hills]. Can you imagine the four of us sitting at a table? I kept wondering if the women were looking over at our table, saying, "Look at the cute guy with Tom Cruise and Warren Beatty. Who is that other guy with Warren and Tom?"

We had the meeting, and we all got along great. That night or the next night, I was invited to dinner at Warren Beatty's house. I was very nervous to have dinner at Warren Beatty's house. It was Warren and his wife, Annette, Rob Reiner and his wife, Michelle, and a few other couples, people that you would recognize. The dinner conversation was very lively. I thought the best thing for me to do during this conversation was not to say a whole lot; I could only make mistakes. But somehow the subject of the moon came up. And I had been kicking the idea around in my mind for a little while of writing a new play about the moon—a historical drama about our journey to the moon. So there were a couple of things I knew about it, and when there was just a moment where it was absolutely appropriate for me to add something to the conversation, I did. And I noticed that

Warren was really looking at me and listening to me closely. When I finished, he said, "Did you know that I want to make a movie about the moon?" I said, "No sir, I didn't know. I promise you, I wasn't pitching you." He called the next day and said, "Listen, instead of doing this political thing that we were talking about, I want you to write me this movie where I go into space." That became our project for the next couple of months. We talked every day, had dinners.

FROUG: Are you paid meanwhile?

SORKIN: I would be. For the moment, Warren was trying to make a deal with Castle Rock. But Castle Rock and Warren weren't able to make a deal with each other. Here's where *The American President* was born. Right at that moment, Warren said to me, "Well, listen, to hell with Rob and Castle Rock. Come with me and make this moon movie." And Rob said to me, "Listen, to hell with Warren and his movie. Come with me and let's do the political movie that we wanted to do." That political movie that we wanted to do was going to change dramatically because of a meeting we would have with Robert Redford.

Rob Reiner and I met with Redford at his offices in Rockefeller Center in New York while Redford was directing *Quiz Show*. Redford said that, for the past ten years, he had been trying to develop at Universal a film where he gets to play a widowed president of the United States who falls in love while he is in office. Redford hauled out a carton of fourteen, sixteen, eighteen scripts written by major screenwriters—terrific writers. There were scripts called *The President Elopes*, *A Candidate Steps Out*, *The State of Our Union*, and all kinds of things. Redford said

"Redford hauled out a carton of fourteen, sixteen, eighteen scripts written by major screenwriters— terrific writers."

that he had been unsuccessful in getting any of them going, and asked if I would be interested in taking a stab at a rewrite: "Just stick your hand in there and pull out a script and rewrite it, any one you choose." I said, "You know, sir, I wouldn't actually want to rewrite someone else's script right now." I was at the top of my game, and I wasn't really in the mood to tie my hands with somebody else's work.

FROUG: You wanted to write your own stuff?

SORKIN: My own. But casting Robert Redford as a widowed president of the United States sounded really interesting to me. I sure liked that idea, but I wanted to go off on my own and write something. He asked me what was going to happen. I told him, "Sir, I can't tell you what the story is going be. I have no idea. You are going to have to let me work on it." Rob Reiner kind of interrupted and said, "Bob, here's how he has to work: You just have to give him his head for a year, a year and a half. We will give him money. I swear he'll come back with a screenplay." And that's what happened. We made a deal, and I went away. And I climbed the walls.

FROUG: At last you were getting paid?

SORKIN: I was indeed getting paid. I have never worked on spec, except for *A Few Good Men*. The play was the only thing I've ever written on my own.

     I went away, and I came back with *The American President*. But it was a little more complicated than that, because most of the time it takes me to write something is spent simply climbing the walls—just thinking about it, trying desperately to think of what it is and what's going to happen. I spent some time doing

". . . most of the time it takes me to write something is spent simply climbing the walls—just thinking about it. . . ."

research at the White House. I spent a lot of time reading. But there was absolutely no story—nothing going on. Months and months were going by. But such was Rob Reiner's confidence in me that he had green-lit the movie and committed to direct it without my having written anything yet. This was Rob's next movie, and sixty million dollars were committed to it. So there was a certain amount of pressure on me to come up with something. Months and months were going by, and Rob was calling me with the "How's it going?" phone calls. I'd tell him "It's going great," as I always do when they call. It was maybe a year before I suddenly was able to start writing. The thing is, when I am suddenly able to start writing, the dam bursts. It's a really fantastic feeling. It's a feeling that I live for. I had come up with the first scene. It was the first thing in the morning, and I was going to follow the president from his bedroom through the walk that he takes to the Oval Office, with various characters crossing his path along the way. All of a sudden the speed and the sense of this thing were coming to me and I was going great guns. I was on page ninety when Rob called next and said, "How's it going?" I said, "Rob, it's going great," and I meant it this time. I said, "I am on page ninety." Now, page ninety usually means that you're thirty pages from the end. So Rob said, "Fantastic! I am going to fly you out here and put you up at the Four Seasons Hotel, which is just a couple of blocks from the office. Every day you can just run the day's pages on over here as you finish. I can be there as your advisor."

FROUG: Where were you?

SORKIN: I was in New York City, where I lived till just a couple of years ago when I got married.

FROUG: So then what happened?

SORKIN: I said, "Great." And it would have been great had it been a normal screenplay. When you are on page ninety of a normal first draft of a screenplay, you are thirty pages from the end. But the first draft of *The American President* turned out to be 385 pages long. I lived at the Four Seasons Hotel for fifteen months. So now it had taken me two and a half years to not finish *The American President* with an almost 400-page first draft. It took so long because the romantic comedy element of it was only one story that was being told in this thing. I absolutely fell in love with the sound of my own voice. I loved being in the White House, and I loved being the president. I was starting and ending wars and fixing the economy and solving all sorts of social problems. It was quite fantastic for me, but for no one else.

FROUG: Did you have access to the White House?

SORKIN: I did. I went several times. I was able to get access through Redford.

FROUG: Who was just on the sidelines?

SORKIN: Redford was on the sidelines because that's where Rob wanted him to be. I wanted Redford much more involved. Rob and Redford would eventually have a falling-out, and Redford would leave the movie. But then we were very lucky to get Michael Douglas at the eleventh hour.

FROUG: At what point did you realize that you were telling a love story?

SORKIN: Well, it was really Rob Reiner who said, "You know, Aaron, this other stuff is great, but what you have to do now is go through the script and just take out everything that doesn't have to do with this love story." It was painful, but I did.

FROUG: But it wasn't painful enough to drive you away from project?

SORKIN: Nothing would be painful enough to drive me away from the project.

FROUG: You had invested too much time writing it.

SORKIN: That's right.

FROUG: Were you happy with the picture?

SORKIN: Very, very happy with the picture.

FROUG: You are at the top of your game in features, and suddenly you're the executive producer of *Sports Night* on TV. And you're writing almost every episode.

SORKIN: Writing every episode. I wrote all twenty-three this year.

FROUG: How the hell do you do that?

SORKIN: Boy, it has been a very, very hard year. Very gratifying, very challenging, and very tiring. There was no bible on the show. We never sat down and had a story meeting. Each week I just wrote a new play. I would begin thinking about it on Monday, and I would spend four days climbing the walls, trying to think of something. Deadlines are the best motivators. Come Friday, I would just say to myself, "We don't have a show for next week. I have to start writing something." And I would write something. I would finish it Sunday, around dinnertime, and that's when the script would go out to everybody that it needed to go out to. Monday morning we had our table reading. Wednesday we began shooting it. We wrapped very early Saturday morning. We did that twenty-three times in a row.

FROUG: Have you had enough of it, or are you going on with it?

SORKIN: I will be doing the same thing this year.

FROUG: What hooks you to it? I'm sure it's not just the money.

SORKIN: No. It's easy to think that it's the money, but unless you are around for four years, unless you can make a hundred episodes and sell them as a package for syndication, they are not worth much. At this point I would make considerably more money in films. But I just had this idea for something that I felt wasn't for movies.

I love writing. I didn't want to just write the pilot and walk away, just create the show and let it go. I wanted to have a longer relationship with it. The show has an unusual voice and cannot be written by a team. With film, you write something by yourself, and then there is the very mechanical, nuts-and-bolts process of making the film, shooting the film, and editing it. You feel good on that opening weekend when there's hoopla surrounding it. That's the milk and cookies aspect, but it goes away so fast. It seems like, gee whiz, that was a couple of year's work for a party I went to one night. It feels remarkably unsatisfying, especially because once you finish writing something, you all of a sudden feel qualified to write it. Now I know how this works. I could really write the hell out of it now. So I wanted to try this for a year or two.

FROUG: That's the best argument I've heard for writing a TV series. Are you going to do more series?

SORKIN: I am not only going on to a second year with *Sports Night*, but I have a new television show, *The West Wing*, which NBC will announce next Monday.

FROUG: Is this an outgrowth of those two hundred first-draft pages of *The American President* that you had to cut? Was this inspired by that screenplay?

SORKIN: No. Although the fact that I enjoyed my experience writing *The American President* as much as I did was certainly a factor in my wanting to set more stories in the White House.

FROUG: You're going to write two series?

SORKIN: Yeah. I realize it's going to be a problem. I don't know how it's going to work, but somehow it will happen.

FROUG: Are you going to build a staff whether you like it or not?

SORKIN: I will build a staff, whether I like it or not, at both shows. It will, at least, get twenty-four scripts, and I can rewrite and polish them rather than having to start from scratch.

FROUG: Has television become more exciting than movies?

SORKIN: I won't say that. I will say that television is just what I am doing right now and I am very, very excited by it. I would think, probably at the end of this coming year, I'll go back to screenwriting.

FROUG: Did you imagine this level of success in both feature films and television while you were a student at Syracuse University?

SORKIN: I was prepared for quite a bit at Syracuse University. I had wonderful teachers there. It's where I really learned how to write. It's where I learned what a play is. It's really where my fire

"I will say that television is just what I am doing right now and I am very, very excited by it."

was lit. But institutional theater, academic theater, when you are in college, is not NFL football. What you play in college is a little bit different, but it ought to be a little bit different.

FROUG: As a kid, did you know you were going to be a writer?

SORKIN: Interestingly, I never wanted to be anything other than an actor. I never wanted to be a fireman or an astronaut. I only ever wanted to be an actor. I was always acting in school plays. I grew up in a suburb just outside New York City, and on the weekends, I would take my allowance money and take a train into the city, where I would see second acts of plays because I couldn't afford to buy a ticket for the whole thing. It was summertime, and I'd wait at a matinee for the audience to pour out onto the sidewalk to buy a pretzel at intermission, and then I would go back in with them and find whatever empty seat there was or stand at the back. I saw the second act of every play you can think of. I have never seen a first act of these plays. As I got a little bit older, I asked my parents if I could take acting class in New York. So I studied acting at Circle in the Square, with Lee Strasberg and Stella Adler. And when I went to Syracuse University, it was as an actor, it was to get a bachelor of fine arts degree in musical theater.

FROUG: Were you a singer?

SORKIN: I sang and I danced. I graduated high school in 1979, and at that time there were only three colleges in the country that offered a BFA in musical theater: Syracuse, Carnegie Mellon in Pittsburgh, and the Boston Conservatory of Music. I auditioned for Syracuse, got in, and was trained to perform. When I graduated in 1983, I moved to New York to begin the life of an unemployed actor. I began auditioning for everything.

"I never wanted to be a fireman or an astronaut. I only ever wanted to be an actor."

When I was twenty-one or twenty-two, I traveled through the South with a touring children's theater company called The Traveling Playhouse. When I say the South, we weren't playing in Atlanta, we were playing Jasper, Alabama. We'd do six or seven shows in elementary school gymnasiums at about ten o'clock in the morning, then pile into a station wagon and a van carrying the costumes and sets. We did *The Wizard of Oz*, *Rip Van Winkle*, and *Greensleeves*. We were paid thirty dollars a performance.

Then I worked with an Equity company for thirty dollars a performance and another twenty-five dollars per diem. And that twenty-five dollars per diem was like gold. You did whatever you could to preserve that twenty-five dollars. You could double or triple your money if three stayed together in very cheap motel rooms. And if you could make it as far as Tennessee, you tried to get back to New York in one night to save that one more night of staying over.

I was in one of these roadside motels, a Motel Six or something in God-knows-where, Georgia. As the trucks rumbled by on the highway outside, I don't know why, I all of a sudden felt like Sam Shepard. I felt like I ought to be writing something. That's the first time that thought went into my head, and it just kept nagging at me. I just felt like a writer without ever having written anything, believe me, up to that point.

Writing, for me, was a chore to be gotten through for an English class. I had no interest in it at all. In fact, I'll tell you a story as an example of how alien that whole idea of being a writer was to me. In my last year in college, I was what was called the "student rep," the drama department liaison to the faculty. One of the more pleasant responsibilities of this job is to organize what is called "Marathon," a series of sketches that are put on on the last day to say goodbye to the outgoing seniors and to let the freshmen know that they are not plebes anymore. So I wrote some of these sketches, and at the big party afterwards, which is everything you can imagine on the last day of an intense four years, one of the faculty members came up to me and said, "Aaron, that was really wonderful. You could do this professionally." And, honestly, I did not know what he meant. "I don't understand," I told him. "You want me to get a job going from college to college organizing parties? For God's sake, I am an actor! What are you talking about?"

So now it's a rainy Friday night in New York City, where I'm living off my children's theater income. I'm actually living on the floor of my ex-girlfriend's studio apartment, where, for fifty dollars a week, she let me pull a futon out on the floor and sleep. She was away for the weekend. Everybody I knew was away for the weekend. It was one of those Friday nights that only happen in New York. One of those nights where you are convinced that everybody in the world has been invited to a party that you have not been invited to. Well, this friend who I grew up with, David, a very successful journalist, had his grandfather's manual typewriter with him for some reason. David was going out of town for the weekend with his girlfriend and did not want to schlep the typewriter around, so he said, "Hey, Aaron, can I just drop this off at your apartment? I'll come pick it up Sunday when I come back to the city." I said, "Sure." So there I was on this miserable, lonely, Manhattan Friday night with just four walls and my friend's grandfather's manual typewriter. There was paper. I don't know where it came from, but I stuck a piece of it into the typewriter and, for the first time ever, wrote dialogue.

You have to imagine how powerful a feeling it was. Suddenly, right out of the box, I felt a confidence that I had never felt in my entire life. All of a sudden everything in the world made sense to me. I thought about how, when I was little, I took out of our local public library an original cast album of *Who's Afraid of Virginia Woolf?* I am sure that at whatever age I was, I did not understand *Who's Afraid of Virginia Woolf?*, but the dialogue was absolutely music to me, like listening to a symphony. I loved dialogue. The same thing had happened when my parents took me to see *That Championship Season*, a wonderful, wonderful play. Just the sound of the dialogue was fantastic to me. Now here I was, just trying to re-create these sounds that I loved so much. I was like a little kid who has an innate sense for the piano but doesn't have enough musical training yet; he's trying to make the sounds that he loves so much, and once someone comes along and teaches him music, he is going to be right there. That was how I became a writer.

FROUG: How did you happen to write *A Few Good Men*? You weren't in the Marine Corps, were you?

SORKIN: No, I was never in the military, but my sister was. I have an older sister, Deborah, who graduated from Boston University Law School and badly wanted to be a trial lawyer. But at the time, she had a terrible confidence problem. She had very good grades in law school, but was terribly shy and didn't do well in interviews. My father is a very successful lawyer and was able to open a lot of doors for her. She went on hundreds of interviews

"I was like a little kid who has an innate sense for the piano but doesn't have enough musical training yet. . ."

but was simply not inspiring confidence, certainly not for being a litigator, someone who needs to go into a courtroom and argue. She was told that she should go into matrimonial law, but it just wasn't what she wanted to do. Then someone said to her, "Have you thought about either the Air Force or Navy Judge Advocate General's Corps?" My sister is the last person in the world who you would ever imagine signing up with a military outfit. Nonetheless, her interest was kind of piqued. She said, "What do you mean?" They told her, "Listen, it's not what you think. You would be able to work in Washington for three years. You get paid thirty-two thousand dollars a year and you can get trial experience right away, and maybe after three years of 'yes, ma'am' and 'no, ma'am; you can be commissioned as a lieutenant junior grade. Right off the bat, you are going to get some confidence. It might be good for you."

My sister checked it out. She joined the Navy Judge Advocate General's Corps. We couldn't believe it. Debbie went off to Newport for officer's training school. My God, what a strange life this is. And there, she was handling petty bicycle thieves and ten dollars' worth of marijuana and that kind of thing. She had been doing that for about ten months when she called me one day and said, "Aaron, you are never going to believe where I am going tomorrow. I am going to our base in Guantanamo Bay, Cuba. Ten marines broke into the barracks room of a platoon mate of theirs, tied him up, and stuffed a rag down his throat." The guy in real life didn't die. She also told me, "These marines are claiming that they did it all because their platoon leader ordered them to." I said, "Debbie, these guys sound terrible. They should hang them from the highest yardarm in the Navy." She said, "Aaron, I am one of the people defending them." So I became very interested in what was going on down there.

FROUG: There was a story.

SORKIN: Yeah, absolutely.

FROUG: So you went down there?

SORKIN: I didn't go down there. I have never been down there. Actually, I quickly lost interest in the real story and began making up my own, because the real-life story was about this poor kid who didn't belong there and was hazed and treated terribly. He was writing a lot of letters to people, asking to get out. Ultimately, this tragedy happens. Every time I thought of the real-life story, it felt to me an awful lot like something we had seen before. It just felt like every TV movie we had ever seen about hazing and that kind of thing.

   I had all sorts of paperwork on the case. Anything that my sister was allowed to show me, she would show me. One day, when I was home, I think for Thanksgiving, she showed me a transcript from something called an Article Thirty-two hearing, which is roughly the military equivalent of a grand jury hearing. They assess the evidence and decide if any charges should be brought. I remember saying to my sister, "Debbie, it seems like this is kind of a sensitive case. Wouldn't you think that, with these Marines claiming that they were given an order and whatnot to beat up one of their own, there'd be more to it than what we've heard about these hazing rituals called code reds? It seems like the government went out of its way to assign very green lawyers to the defense and very big-time lawyers to the prosecution. Why would they do something like that?"

I've never forgotten what my sister said. It's a line in the play. It's a line in the movie. She said, "Probably to make sure it never saw the inside of a courtroom." And I thought, "Now we are in business. Forget about the kid. The kid's dead at the beginning in my version. This thing is about the lawyers who were brought in." Anytime you have a story about an ordinary person in an extraordinary situation, you are in business.

FROUG: You certainly turned it into a terrific story. What would you advise kids who want to be screenwriters?

"I would advise kids, first of all, not to neglect anything else about life."

SORKIN: I would advise kids, first of all, not to neglect anything else about life. One of my biggest regrets is that I never got a liberal arts education; I went right into a conservatory program. I would tell them to keep their eyes open, study hard, and keep living their lives. But I would also tell them to watch a lot of movies and read a lot of screenplays. Read screenplays, don't just watch movies. In fact, read everything. Read as much as you can and write as much as you can.

I'll tell you a story. I was in a playwrights' unit, Playwrights Horizons in New York City, with four other writers, two of whom had graduated from the playwriting program at Yale. I am terribly envious and terribly jealous of anyone who graduated from the playwriting program at Yale. I always wished I had graduated from that program. One day I asked one of these guys, "What, exactly, did you learn there? Please tell me. I am sure there is some gap in my education. What do they teach you in a playwriting program at Yale?" He said, "A lot of the same stuff they taught you in your BFA program at Syracuse—theater history, play analysis, scene construction. You read a lot of plays; you talk about a lot of plays. But," he added, "the best thing about doing it is that it gives you an opportunity to write the worst plays you are ever going to write. And you get to write them without the pressure of paying the rent, getting the *New York Times* critic's approval, worrying whether the star is going to like it, or wondering why you're doing it. You get to write without any consequences at all, and writing is not that different from playing the violin—you've got to practice." So I would say to a young man or woman who wants to be a writer, "Practice. Write all the time."

[Author's note: Since our interview, Aaron Sorkin's one-hour weekly television drama, *The West Wing*, has debuted to almost unanimously laudatory reviews and has been placed on the top-ten lists of critics all across the country. It has received a Peabody Award, and no doubt many Emmys are waiting in the wings. Sorkin has written or co-written every episode to date; he is also co-executive producer of the series. In the opinion of this writer, *The West Wing* is arguably the best-written dramatic series in the history television. I urge aspiring screenwriters to watch Sorkin's work to see how sharply characters can be etched and how much emotional power and character development can be generated with but a few lines of dialogue. It is dramatic writing at its best.]

FILMOGRAPHY

1992   *A Few Good Men*, based on his Broadway play

1993   *Malice* (shared credit)

1994   *The American President*

1995   *Sports Night*, television series, creator, writer, executive producer

1996   *The West Wing*, television series, creator, writer, co-executive producer

Get Scotty!

An Interview with

Scott Frank

"I think the young screenwriter should forget about trying to "get in" and should focus entirely on being a good writer, because no one who has ever given me a script, who is a good writer, hasn't gotten into the business. There are a lot of talented people who try it and give up, but those with talent, passion, discipline, and commitment are already screenwriters. You are already going to get in; it's going to happen."

—Scott Frank

Seeing the extraordinary work of one screenwriter in recent years ignited my desire to undertake the writing of this sequel to *Zen and the Art of Screenwriting* almost as much any other factor. This writer is turning conventional structure on its head and inside out. He can trick audiences as no one since Houdini has, and win their applause in much the same way. Scott Frank, the master showman, is one of the most exciting screenwriting talents to emerge since movies got voices, and he is among today's most sought after and highly paid screenwriters in Hollywood.

Scott Frank's screenwriting style is wonderfully original. You can immediately recognize a Frank screenplay because it blasts out of the starting blocks (the first scene) full of power, fun, and surprises, and nothing in it thereafter is predictable either. His style is often nonlinear: Beginnings are sometimes middles (*Out of Sight*), and his endings are sometimes beginnings (*Get Shorty*). And sometimes he can disorient you so that you don't know where you are in the story (*Dead Again*), but you can't stop watching because you're having a marvelous time and you've got to know what is going to happen next. Frank makes his tricks seem so effortless that you aren't even aware that you're being tricked until well after this master storyteller has sprung yet another surprise—the final trick you expected doesn't turn out to be what you expected.

Like many of his peers, Frank first wrote screenplay after screenplay, steadily improving his art and craft. He is a classic example of the "overnight" star who spent ten years getting to the top. If you study only one screenwriter's work, make that one Scott Frank. You will be learning from the best that the film industry has to offer. Frank's work will teach you to rise above the mob, to be daring and courageous. Those qualities, along with perseverance and determination, will set you free.

Frank is a friendly, charming, and unassuming young man. I taped this conversation with him in his huge loft-style office located in an old brick building in downtown Pasadena.

FROUG: *Dead Again* is arguably the most original screenplay since *Citizen Kane*. Tell me how you created it.

FRANK: It's funny that you say that it's the most original screenplay, because I feel like I just ripped off *Rebecca*.

FROUG: You certainly fooled me.

FRANK: I was fascinated by a book by Otto Friedrich called *City of Nets*, which was basically about Hitler and Stalin and what happened to those great writers and musicians who fled Germany and settled in Hollywood. I was fascinated with those characters and their lives. At the same time, I was doodling around with the idea of writing history, and the ideas sort of came together. I had the title in my head, *Dead Again*. I also had this character of this man who was an heir chaser in my head, and I wanted to write about him.

FROUG: An heir chaser?

FRANK: Yeah, a guy who chases down people who are unaware that they've inherited a lot of money. It actually is a real business. The guy was himself an orphan, a man without an identity. Finding people and locating lost family members was really interesting. Those different ideas all sort of swam around in my head. One day I told my ideas to Dennis Feldman, a screenwriter who was working at Paramount. He really helped me with the story.

FROUG: Synchronizing those ideas?

FRANK: What helped me to join them was the idea I had of telling the story of a man out to locate this woman's identity and the notion of using reincarnation, which is something I have no belief in whatsoever but used as a narrative tool, telling simultaneous stories. I thought that it would be really interesting if the woman he tried to protect had perhaps killed him forty years earlier. That would be an interesting dynamic.

FROUG: Did you expect that Kenneth Branagh would bring in his wife and that they would play both couples?

FRANK: No, it was originally written for four separate actors: two actors in their forties, who were slightly older than the two actors in present day. In fact, in my original idea, the woman in the present day was sixteen, and the man found himself strangely attracted to a teenager. It was kind of messing with all those demons, but ultimately, I decided that that would take it into *Lolita* territory.

FROUG: But it sounds more interesting then Branagh and Emma Thompson playing all four parts, past tense as well as present tense.

FRANK: When he came on as director, he stipulated that he and his wife would each play two parts. That was what he wanted to do.

FROUG: That was part of the deal?

FRANK: Part of the deal.

FROUG: Did that change the script significantly?

FRANK: Yeah, I think it did, because it made the movie more Kenneth's sensibility, which is much more theatrical than mine. And even though he was very faithful to the screenplay, I think the tone of the movie is different from the tone of the script. The tone of the script is a little darker and tougher and sexier. The tone of the movie is, I think, a little more theatrical, almost campy. But I still love the film.

FROUG: *Dead Again* is so different in style from *Little Man Tate* that it hardly seems as if the same screenwriter wrote both.

FRANK: Yes. But the other thing that intrigued me about writing *Dead Again* was my previous script. I found *Little Man Tate* to be very episodic, so I said to myself, "With the next screenplay, I am going to master structure." I really wanted to make my weakness my strength. So I worked very hard at creating a strong structure for *Dead Again*, and I was lucky that I had people like Lindsay Doran and Dennis Feldman, who stayed on also to help me learn about structure. Another thing that I did was read, over and over, *Red Harvest*, which I think has a perfect purpose structure.

FROUG: It certainly isn't the classic paradigm structure.

FRANK: No, but for me, it's perfect mystery structure. In terms of setup and payoff, it ends up linking twenty-some odd murders, and it all makes perfect sense.

FROUG: It's like a circular structure?

FRANK: Yes, it is. I really like that. I did a lot of that.

"I really wanted to make my weakness my strength."

FROUG: It seemed to me that you use the same circular structure in *Out of Sight*.

FRANK: Yes. I feel like it's a great way to have your cake and eat it too. The problem with film is that you can't digress. You can't really tell enough of the character story in film. But if you play with the structure, and if you make the structure work for you, you are not flashing back just to fill in character, it's relevant to the story. You are actually telling the current story by telling the past story. I think it's a way to begin a great character.

FROUG: It's certainly effective. Is your secret withholding information?

FRANK: Yes. I think it's really important to do that. I think it's okay to ask a lot of questions in the first half of the movie as long as you can answer them.

FROUG: But you want to delay answering them as long as possible?

FRANK: Yes. It's compelling, and you want to trick people into thinking they know the answers. The fun for them is that, all along, you are floating things out there that make them think they know the answer, and then you try to fool them later down the road.

FROUG: In *Get Shorty*, of course, the structure is a little different, but it turns out to be a movie within a movie.

FRANK: Right, but only in the last scene.

FROUG: Was that a last-minute idea?

FRANK: No. The problem with *Get Shorty* as a novel was that there was no ending. In fact, the last part of the book is something along the lines of the ending: "Fuckin' endings, man, they aren't

". . . you want to trick people into thinking they know the answers."

as easy as they look." I decided that might be a fun way to end the film, and that's exactly how we pulled it off.

FROUG: It was a big surprise, too. You are a master of surprises. They're your signature.

FRANK: For me, most of the surprises are happy accidents. I feel that if you rewrite a screenplay enough—force yourself to rewrite it enough—those happy accidents will happen and you will discover surprises between the twists and turns. The only way those things will happen is if you have the discipline to rewrite over and over and over.

FROUG: About how many times would you say you rewrite a screenplay?

FRANK: Too many to count. Before I'll even call it a first draft, probably ten to twenty times.

FROUG: Adapting *Get Shorty* or *Out of Sight*, for example, how close to the book do you feel you need to stay or do you want to stay?

FRANK: When you are adapting something, it's really important to find out what it is about for you in terms of the theme or character and where you connect with the material. Otherwise, you're just turning a book into a movie. I need to decide what it is about for me. And anything that doesn't play to that in the novel, I have to lose.

FROUG: Do you approach your adaptations of Elmore Leonard's novels as basically comedy?

FRANK: No. I think that people in Elmore Leonard's stories are very funny, but they don't know they are funny. In fact, they are dead serious. I feel like the comedy in his books comes out of character and not jokes. You have to be very careful not to wink because he's not winking. I think that's the key. You're laughing, but you're not laughing the way you are at a straight-on comedy.

FROUG: The irony is always there. That's what you keep. Do you look for an action line?

FRANK: I probably look for many action lines.

FROUG: That's what seems to emerge. All kinds of stories are being unwound.

FRANK: And they all are telling the same story thematically, but they're certainly divergent stories.

FROUG: How many pages does your first draft have to be?

FRANK: It's a long draft, a 200-page draft. Then I cut things that are obviously not going to work.

FROUG: What are your working hours?

FRANK: I work best early in the morning. I drop my kids off at school and come here and work right away. Say eight-thirty until lunchtime, then I take a couple of hours off in the middle of the day, and then I'll work again for an hour and a half before I go home.

FROUG: Generally, how long do you work on an outline before you are ready to start writing?

FRANK: I will write about something for a long time, anywhere from three to six months. Mostly, I work through character. I really want to know the characters. I am not talking about history; I am talking about who are they, what do they want, what's in their way.

FROUG: What's in their way is kind of critical, isn't it?

FRANK: Absolutely critical. Because you want them to get what they want in the end or not get it in some dramatic way.

FROUG: But along the way, it seems that you constantly have to have them run up against opposition.

FRANK: They should not only run up against opposition, they should also run up against their worst nightmare at all costs.

FROUG: *Get Shorty* is based on an Elmore Leonard novel, with a screenplay by Scott Frank. It stars John Travolta, Gene Hackman, Rene Russo, and Danny DeVito. How does it magically become "a Barry Sonnenfeld film"?

FRANK: We'd have to ask Barry Sonnenfeld, actually. I would be embarrassed to do that. But I don't think the public cares one way or the other.

FROUG: Do you feel that screenwriters have a beef with the Directors Guild for this egomaniacal credit?

FRANK: Once the writers allowed it to happen, the directors are never going to give it back. It's hard to give them the credit and take it away. But if there is some way to make them feel stupid about taking it, then we might get back to sanity.

FROUG: Is there a growing rewrite industry in Hollywood, bringing in one big-name writer to rewrite another big-name writer? Are the movies going to get better or are the studios just protecting the asses of some inexperienced executives?

FRANK: Sometimes you rewrite and it makes the movie better. Sometimes the movie wouldn't get made if a particular writer didn't rewrite the material. Sometimes the movie needs to be rewritten. I think that sometimes the writer doesn't care: The original writer did it and moved on. Sometimes the original writer isn't solving the problems so much as shuffling them around. I have done that with my own work, where I just couldn't lick it.

FROUG: What movie?

FRANK: I think, on *Little Man Tate*, I never quite solved the problems with the screenplay. I loved the movie, and it remains, for me, one of the highlights of my career. But when I look at the script, I see that I never solved all of the problems. There are scripts I put away because I couldn't think about them anymore. *Heaven's Prisoner* certainly is a movie where I never really had enough time to finish. I watch that movie and think it's a first draft that they shot.

FROUG: Do you feel that *Little Man Tate*'s more conventional structure brought you to change your style in your later films?

FRANK: It's my fault, and I blame no one but myself. I think it was my own immaturity at the time. Originally the script was much more surreal. It was a black comedy. The kid with the cape died. Fred replaced him, and it was funny when he died and the way he died. I feel like the movie lost something in an effort to make it more realistic instead of surrealistic. I did not know how to do that. So in some of it, I feel like the writing is a little clumsy, and I feel like the wrap-up is rather abrupt and just not right. I like my earlier drafts better. I like what I did originally. And that's not Jodie Foster's fault, that's my fault.

FROUG: How did you come to be a screenwriter?

FRANK: I just love movies. I think that I loved three things when I was a kid. I loved reading books, I loved watching movies, and I loved writing. As a kid, I always went to see movies and retold them to people. I have a very strong memory for narratives. No one had told me until college that you could write movies and actually earn a living at it.

FROUG: When did you write your first screenplay?

FRANK: I wrote my first full-length screenplay when I was a freshman in college.

FROUG: Did you get good response?

FRANK: Yes, I did. Although it was more like a series of skits than a screenplay.

FROUG: You have a real comic vein running through your work.

FRANK: I think everything, no matter how serious it is, should have a sense of humor. *Ordinary People* has a sense of humor. I think that humor brings into relief the more serious elements, like tension or emotion. And if you take yourself too seriously, no one else will take you seriously.

FROUG: I think there are two things that are thematic to your work: You have an ironic sense of humor and you fracture time so both the story and the characters become unpredictable. The biggest problem most writers have is that they can't generate surprise. You do it constantly.

FRANK: I think they can't generate surprise because they are thinking from the outside in. They are thinking about making up plots—what happens. Plots should come from your characters. Know your people. If you have really great characters, you always

"I think everything, no matter how serious it is, should have a sense of humor."

have too much plot. There are always too many directions to go in. I think that movies have become so conceptual that people start with an idea instead of a character, and then people the idea with attitudes—usually a movie star with a particular attitude. I think it is very hard to surprise people when you work that way.

FROUG: So you start with character?

FRANK: Always, always. If I am stuck in the middle of my screenplay, it's invariably because I don't know the people and there is not an interesting dynamic. I may know this person, but not that person. Therefore, I don't know what the dynamic is between them.

FROUG: When you say you start with the characters, do you need to know what they want and also know what stops them from getting it?

FRANK: Well, I think I know certain obstacles that they are facing. I try to figure out what the conflict is going to be, and I like to know what my ending is ahead of time. I like to know if they are going to get what they want or are they not going to get what they want in some dramatic way.

FROUG: Are you concerned whether they are likable?

FRANK: No. I am just concerned that they are not boring. As long as they are interesting, whether they are likable or not is irrelevant.

FROUG: What would you advise young writers to do to become successful?

FRANK: To write a lot, and to read a lot. Quit watching movies and copying movies. Quit thinking about what sells. Quit thinking about ideas and start thinking about the questions that you, as a writer, care about creatively: What is my point of view? What is

"If I am stuck in the middle of my screenplay, it's invariably because I don't know the people and there is not an interesting dynamic."

my voice? What do I sound like as the writer? If you don't know, you should be mimicking someone you love and respect until you're comfortable enough to discover you own voice. The question I get asked most often is "What do people want?" I have no idea what people want. I have no idea what it is that sells, which is a better way of putting it. But if you write something to sell it, you are already too late. Who knows what's going to sell? It changes every year. I feel that people are not spending enough time thinking, "What will make me a better writer? How can I be a better writer?" Because the truth is the industry will ultimately find you. I really do believe that, and I really do believe that there are very few fresh voices out there. There are a lot of people with ideas, but having a good idea, even if it's a commercial idea, doesn't make you a writer. You'll get replaced. You'll get rewritten. They'll buy your script for that idea, then hire me to rewrite it.

FROUG: Do you do a lot of rewriting?

FRANK: I have done a lot of rewriting. I am trying to do less of it. I bought a house that I couldn't afford in Pasadena. I rewrote my way through the remodel.

FROUG: Are you are working on an original?

FRANK: I just finished an original called *The Lookout* for Dreamworks. I am adapting *Charlie and the Chocolate Factory* for Warner Bros.

FROUG: At the same time?

FRANK: *The Lookout* is completed. I am adapting *Charlie and the Chocolate Factory* while I am writing *Minority Report*, which is an adaptation of a Philip K. Dick story for Dreamworks and Steven Spielberg.

FROUG: How do you bounce your mind back and forth from one script to the other?

FRANK: If I work on a lot of things, I get a better rhythm going. I used to go through this phase where I would agonize over every word. As a result, I began to get very frustrated because I had all these ideas that I wasn't letting go of. It was all about fear. I have a very strong inner critic; I pretty much hate everything I write. Doing rewrites forced me to get over that very quickly, because I didn't have time to think about it. Now I'm finding beauty in imperfection.

FROUG: Maybe your inner critic is what makes you such a tremendous writer.

FRANK: Maybe, but I also think it has become something that gets in the way, because it inhibits me. I think challenging your work and asking the hard questions are valid and necessary to being a good writer, but I think inhibiting yourself is dangerous.

FROUG: How many pages do you do in a good day?

FRANK: It depends on what I'm writing. If I'm writing dialogue, I can write ten pages in a day. But sometimes I may write a paragraph or a half a page and think it's a great day because it's a great half a page.

FROUG: What is your ballpark for finishing a screenplay, time-wise?

FRANK: If I figure in doing other things, my whole messy process is probably about a year for a first draft.

FROUG: Is a deadline a benefit?

FRANK: It is and it isn't. Good writing is as much a series of happy accidents as it is hard work. The more time you have, the more time you have for those happy accidents to occur. You discover things by mistake. I think all the great discoveries have been because someone dropped a vial of something on the floor and it mixed with something else. I feel it's the same way with writing. When I have more time to discover what it's really about, I get to go deeper and deeper and deeper. If, for instance, I had written *Out of Sight* very quickly, I don't think I would have found that structure. But sometimes I can also overwork something; I can start to do damage.

FROUG: How should a young screenwriter go about getting into the business?

FRANK: I think the young screenwriter should forget about trying to "get in" and should focus entirely on being a good writer, because no one who has ever given me a script, who is a good writer, hasn't gotten into the business. There are a lot of talented people who try it and give up, but those with talent, passion, discipline and commitment are already screenwriters. They are already going to get in; it's going to happen. Sooner or later they're going to meet the right person, who will hand it to someone else, who is going to hand it to someone else.

When it comes to screenwriting, it's the writing. You don't hear people who want to play professional tennis ask to be introduced to the head of Wimbledon. No, they're out there hitting a thousand forehands and a thousand backhands. But for some reason, in the case of screenwriting, people don't think that way. The format makes it appear deceptively easy. If they can type something up in the format that has a beginning, middle and end, and has some dialogue in between, they think they've written a screenplay. But if you're a writer with an original voice,

"I think the young screenwriter should forget about trying to 'get in' and should focus entirely on being a good writer. . . ."

[53]

and with those other four qualities I just mentioned, somehow, some way, the world is going to find you.

FILMOGRAPHY

1991	*Little Man Tate*
1991	*Dead Again*
1993	*Malice* (shared credit)
1995	*Get Shorty* (adaptation of the novel by Elmore Leonard)
1996	*Heaven's Prisoners* (shared credit)
1998	*Out of Sight* (adaptation of the novel by Elmore Leonard)

"You write a hit play the same way you write a flop."
— William Saroyan

*"If you don't fall on your ass every once in a while,
you're not really trying."*
— Sol Saks, *Funny Business*

*"There are only three reasons why you should leave a line in a finished
script. Three. No more. (1) It' s funny. (2) It's a plot development. (3) It's
character development. And an ideal line would do all three at once."*
— Brian Cooke, *Writing Comedy for Television*

*". . . the very nicest thing Hollywood can possibly say to a writer is that he
is too good to be only a writer."*
— Raymond Chandler

Grabbing at Straws

Many aspiring screenwriters eagerly seek teachers who can make screenwriting appear easy. Be warned: All but one or two of these eagerly sought make-it-easy folk share a common trait—they are not themselves screenwriters. Some even boast of their lack of professional experience (and talent), assuring their audiences that they therefore have "objectivity." They also often explain that they don't write and sell million-dollar screenplays because they're "too busy" telling others how to do it. They epitomize George Bernard Shaw's dictum: "Those who can, do. Those who can't, teach." And they lead you to believe that screenwriting is all about structure and little else. One of the most famous of these teachers tells his students that you can't teach talent: "Either you've got it or you don't." What non-sense! What he might have said is that you can't teach talent in a one- or two-day moneymaking seminar.

Teach talent? You bet! Most great artists, through hard work and self-discipline, *teach* themselves to achieve greatness. The art world, as well as the movie world, is filled with extraordinary people who *taught* themselves until they developed their art—their talent.

An example: My former student the late Jeffrey Boam had seem-ingly little talent for screenwriting when he decided he had to be a screenwriter. The first screenplays he showed me, when he applied for admission to my class, were in standard screenplay form, with conventional three-act structures, but they were snoozes. I told him that based on those scripts, I could not accept him into my class. But Jeffrey was not to be dissuaded. He kept writing screenplay after screenplay, improving himself, *creating* his talent, until he became the highest-paid contract screenwriter on record. (Over our last lunch together in L.A., we laughed at his meager beginning.)

Jeffrey Boam's talent was self-motivated and self-created. I always mention him to those who state, "Either you have it or you don't." When he started, he had no illusions that he was or would ever become a great screenwriter. Still, he worked and developed himself, never losing his humility or sense of humor. Alas, Jeffrey's life was cut much too short by an extremely rare disease. He died as he lived, with courage and dignity. I admired and loved him.

Another example: My former student Beth Sullivan, who put herself through UCLA film school by working full time as a waitress, showed only a hint of her talent during our seminars at UCLA. But she had the nothing-will-stand-in-my-way determination to develop herself into a strong writer. It came as no surprise to me that she went on to write one outstanding TV movie after another, winning awards and recognition while writing in support of controversial and socially significant causes. She also created *Dr. Quinn, Medicine Woman*, which remained a top-rated television drama for many years. For this series, which she produced, Beth wrote or rewrote all of the scripts. I don't believe that such talent was her gift at birth. She developed her talent through hard work, *teaching* herself to be a class-act writer. By any measure, Beth Sullivan is a successful writer. Hers is an important voice that will be seen and heard for years to come.

Was she born with talent? I don't know. But I do know that by hard work she developed her talent.

You can't develop talent in a weekend seminar or a single semester of college. It is what a writer can only, over time, develop for himself or herself. When you focus your attention only on the quick fix of structure, you are grabbing at straws, avoiding the hardest work of all: *teaching yourself to write*. I know from many firsthand experiences as a writer, producer, and teacher that people who dedicate themselves to the task can and do develop talent, sometimes exceptional talent. Focus your attention on developing your art, your talent. The eternal truth is that there is only one person who can make it happen, and that person is you. Only a con man or a self-serving fool will ever tell you that it's easy.

By the way, structure is a piece of cake. For those who are looking for guidance on structure without "painting by the numbers," I offer this advice: The best structure escalates dramatic tension by creating new and surprising developments. If you've fully explored your characters in depth, they will do both of these things for you. The key: Create exciting characters, find their conflicts, and put them to work for you. Dull screenplays come from dull characters.

Getting Even

The meeting, like all faculty meetings, was boring. I was the new kid on the UCLA Theater Arts, Film & Television Department's writing faculty. I had been hired as a lecturer on a one-year trial basis. My job in my first faculty meeting was to listen, learn, and keep my mouth shut.

A distinguished, articulate professor of filmmaking had the floor. He was explaining why he taught his young filmmakers that they were the "auteurs" of their films. "The truth is, writers are carpenters," he said. "You tell them what you want; they do it. The vision is entirely the director's."

To a man, the film production faculty nodded in agreement. I could not believe my eyes and ears. Swallowing hard, I said nothing. However, when the meeting adjourned, I approached the good professor. "Do you really believe that writers are carpenters?" I asked him. "I certainly do," he replied with a patronizing smile, "but please take no offense. I just believe that film is a director's medium and that writing has an important but minor role in it."

I said no more because I didn't relish talking to a wall.

By the time I got home, I had already written, in my mind, a proposal for a book I called *The Screenwriter Looks at the Screenwriter*, a collection of interviews with some of Hollywood's best screenwriters. I would show the professor and all the other know-nothings teaching in film schools that they were not only wrong but also boneheaded. Fueled by my simmering anger, not at the professor, who was actually a very nice guy, but at the demeaning claptrap being taught to students, I needed all of an hour to write my book proposal.

I showed my proposal to my good friend the late Arthur Knight, then a professor at USC's film school, where for seven years I had been teaching as an adjunct professor. Arthur liked it. He phoned his book agent in New York and asked her to read it. (Knight was a true gentlemen and among the most knowledgeable film teachers on the planet.) His agent, Betty Anne Clarke, liked the idea, but said it would be a tough sell: "Nobody is really interested in screenwriters."

A couple of months later she phoned with the news that she'd found a publisher, Macmillan, that would publish it in hardback. She said that she especially liked the young editor who would be working with me.

The editor phoned the next day, full of enthusiasm, wanting to know how soon I could start sending him interview transcripts. I told him that I would go to work immediately.

Indeed I did. Most of the screenwriters I would be interviewing were old friends, and I had worked with a couple of them. Piece of cake. Within two weeks I had my first three interviews completed, and the rest lined up. As I had expected, it was more fun than work.

Then one day I got a call from my young editor. He had bad news: "I quit," he said. "I hate my job. I'm going to drive a cab if necessary. Another editor will take over, so just keep doing what you're doing. He'll give you a call soon."

Weeks passed before I heard from the new editor. When he did call, he got straight to the point. "Frankly," he said, "I have very little interest in screenwriters. I voted against your book. But what the hell, send me the transcripts and I'll see what I can do with them."

Not long after that I sent him all the interview transcripts. Then I waited. Months passed without a response. I was where all writers spend a lot of their time—limbo.

Finally he called. "Sorry I haven't gotten back to you. I've been as busy as the devil. Next fall we're going to publish your book pretty much as is. Were I to work on these transcripts, there's no telling how much I would cut. Why don't you take a whack at it? Trim them wherever you can and send me back your copy. By the way, I really liked your introduction." That was the last I heard from him.

On publication, the book received a couple of fairly good reviews merely making note that somebody had said something good about screenwriters, and that it was probably a good idea that someone did. One Sunday morning, weeks after the book came out, I opened the *New York Times* Arts & Leisure section, and there, on the front page, was my introduction to *The Screenwriter Looks at the Screenwriter*, reprinted in its entirety without comment!

Ironically, among the first people at UCLA to congratulate me was the professor whose remarks had unwittingly started me on my screenwriting book career. He said, "Bill, you taught me something."

The book was published without fanfare. Soon it vanished beneath the waves like a leaky canoe. However, Macmillan did show a kind of interest in the book: For years they continued to send me semiannual negative royalty statements, advising me of how poorly the volume was selling and how much money they had lost by giving me a $2,500 advance. My heart bled for them.

Another grousing writer story, right? Wrong. It's a phoenix story of life rising from the ashes. Cut to twenty-five years later, when I receive a phone call from Gwen Feldman. She says, "I like *The Screenwriter Looks at the Screenwriter*. My company, Silman-James Press, would like to reprint it." Then, as icing on the cake, she adds, "We'd like you to do a follow-up book, interviewing the new crop of young screenwriters. Are you interested?" What a question!

For those who are counting, this is now my fifth screenwriting book for Silman-James. (I later learned that Feldman is Silman and James is Jim Fox, who turned out to be my editor as well as copublisher.) That first phone call from Gwen ten years ago was the impetus for five books. The intervening years have been surprisingly productive, and my relationship with Silman-James Press has been warm, friendly, and mutually fruitful.

Why am I telling this story to aspiring writers? It contains a very important lesson: You can use your anger, which is a negative energy, and make it positive by telling yourself, "I'll show those bastards!"

No Laughing Matter

One of my former screenwriting students once presented me with a half-finished melodrama about a reporter going after a big political scandal. He and I both knew that it didn't work—it was going nowhere. In fact, he began to make jokes about it, which prompted me to remark offhandedly, "Why don't you make it a comedy?"

Before the quarter was over, he handed me a completed screenplay with the uncertain comment, "Maybe it's funny."

That night I had a screenplay reading such as I had never known before. I no sooner started page one, scene one, than I began to laugh out loud. Pretty soon my guffaws were shaking me out of my chair while my tears of laughter kept me grabbing for Kleenex. Although the last act was weak, it mattered little. This guy had an unparalleled comedy-writing talent. And there was not a joke in the screenplay—the laughter emerged from the behavior of the characters and their ironic comments.

Within a relatively short time after graduation, this young comedy writer, a million-a-year contract in hand, was writing for a sitcom production company. From that point on, he has moved from hit comedy series to hit comedy series, always pulling in bountiful salaries. The last time I visited his home, his small children were running around the house, gleefully laughing and shouting, "Funny is money! Funny is money!" Their proud, beaming father pulled me aside and said, "I taught them that."

Where does such unique talent come from? I think it arises out of the writer's own personal pain and his or her ability to see the absurdity and irony in all human behavior. For the gifted comedy writer, a sense of the absurd and a sense of irony, not jokes, are the keys to writing funny.

Are you a comedy writer? To find out, simply ask yourself if life's absurdities give you an inner laugh. If they do, you should try your hand at comedy. If your friends laugh when you talk and tell you that you're funny, and if you know they are being truthful, pay attention to them. If your siblings (forget mom and dad, they're too easy an audience) laugh at your offhand remarks, by all means try writing comedy.

Take a story you've been working on and see how it would play if you turned it upside down and wrote it funny. Any drama can be turned into a comedy. Browse through Neil Simon's memoir, *Rewrites*, and you will discover that history's most famous and successful comedy writer boasts that he does not write jokes.

If you watch TV sitcoms, you already know how desperate they are for comedy writers. In most homes in America today, the laughter heard in the TV room is coming from the laugh track, not the viewers. If you can generate laughter off the printed page, your career is made. You can begin by sending a script to the producers of your favorite sitcom. When you do, always enclose a cover letter that in and of itself is funny. By the way, choose a show that you believe is apt to last through one season. That may be harder than writing the script.

"You tell the story whatever way it comes out. . . . I mean, I would rather risk boring an audience in the first ten or fifteen minutes than have to catch up in the middle and explain what was going on because I wanted a racy opening. . . . Generally speaking, if you don't set everything up in the beginning, you'll pay for it in the middle or in the end. So I would rather pay for it at the beginning. It's not television, and they're not going to go off into the icebox or they're not going to change channels. An audience in a movie will forgive you for just about anything for the first ten minutes or so. But really nothing at the end."

— Robert Towne, from *Word Into Image*
(courtesy of American Film Foundation)

Inside the Mind of the Master

An Interview with

Frank Pierson

"In general, people either have the physical facility for mixing the paints or they don't. Some people have an ear or they don't. It's almost like saying that either you can write or you can't write. That doesn't mean you can't learn to write, in the sense that you have to keep trying to do it and do it over and over again until it begins to come to you more and more naturally. But the really important thing about writing is how to think about writing, how to think about the characters that are in your piece—who they are and what it is they want."

—Frank Pierson

Frank Pierson has probably influenced more of today's generation of screenwriters than any other writer in his field, and he is on most screenwriters' very short list of the greatest screenwriters of all time. Scott Frank told me that he became interested in screenwriting after he saw Pierson's *Dog Day Afternoon*. Brian Helgeland told me that Pierson's *Cool Hand Luke* turned him on to screenwriting. It is no accident that this elder statesman of screenwriters has won an Oscar and received multiple Oscar nominations for his screenplays and kudos from critics and audiences alike for his directing.

Frank and I first met in 1956, when he was a reporter covering the Hollywood beat for *Time* and *Life* magazines. Over lunch in a Mexican restaurant across the street from Paramount Studios, we talked about our futures. I was a newly hired writer-producer under contract to Screen Gems, the television arm of Columbia Pictures; Pierson was interested in becoming a TV writer.

After Frank penned a few scripts for popular TV series, his career took off like a rocket. He wrote himself from triumph to triumph, winning recognition awarded few screenwriters. The Writers Guild of America has bestowed on him the Valentine Davies Award, the Edmund H. North Award, and its highest of all honors for a lifetime of outstanding work, the Screen Laurel Award. Frank was also twice elected president of the Writers Guild of America, west, and is presently artistic director of the American Film Institute and a member of the Sundance Institute's teaching staff.

Our discussions about screenwriting and the peculiar nature of our work have been going on in one form or another for more decades than either of us wishes to count. Forty-three years after our first lunch together we recorded the following interview. Frank remains lean and handsome but noticeably mellowed.

FROUG: Tell me about your struggle in writing *Dog Day Afternoon*.

PIERSON: Wow. What can I tell you? It was a struggle from the start because it wasn't really a story. The plot was there in terms of a crime that was committed: Somebody went into a bank. They toted a gun. The people in the bank reacted. Hostages were held. The police came. And, at the end, one of the bank robbers was shot. So there was a sequence of events that consisted of an existential plot, as it were. Then there was a cast of characters— the police officers, the FBI people, the people in the bank, the robbers. Why did the robbers go into the bank in the first place? What were their motives? They were not just guys who needed money for drugs or one thing or another. There was an underlying motive, which was to buy a sex change operation for the homosexual wife of the lead bank robber. All interesting stuff, but how do you organize that for a screenplay?

It was also about the crowd effect and all the things that happened around that. Thousands of people tuned in on television. It was one of the very first crimes where the news media had flexibility. They had new lighting equipment. And they had developed just enough skill to be actually able to be on the scene—to film the people, to call in to the bank, to actually put visuals of the people in the bank on television. That sort of thing had never happened before. So that was an important aspect of it.

"Figuring out what the movie was about became less important, finally, than getting to know who the character was who went into that bank and pulled guns on people. . . ."

Figuring out what the movie was about became less important, finally, than getting to know who the character was who went into that bank and pulled guns on people, threatened them, held them under duress for many hours, and induced them to act in a sense of generosity of spirit. He had a sympathy with them that induced them to react as though they were on his team and against the police. It was among the earliest instances of what was later to become known as the Stockholm syndrome. All these things were new to the police. They were not skilled in hostage situations, and hostage negotiators were a concept that was only developed by the police after this incident happened in the 1970s.

So there was all this mishmash of extraordinary material for what the movie was about. We could begin writing it in a lot of different ways. I interviewed everybody involved. But the one person I was never able to meet was John Wojtowicz, the actual bank robber. They called him Sonny in the movie, a terrible name. But the questions were: Who was Sonny? What made him go there and behave the way he did? Why did he induce people to respond to him in the way they did? I struggled with this for months. I literally was in despair, and I just couldn't figure out what to write because I couldn't organize the material in the order in which the information should come up, only in the actual timeline of what happened, which was not all that interesting because it was very random. It had no dramatic structure to it. It had no narrative drive. It just was one thing after another: They did this and then they did that and then they did the other thing. In the real-life situation, everybody was just trying to cope with the minutiae of the experience without any kind of overall thematic structure. That's the difference between real life and art. Art is a matter of providing a kind of structure. It provides the kind of meaning that's read for understanding, that unravels as we go along through the story.

FROUG: The theme?

PIERSON: The theme. It took me a very long time. I almost called my agent to ask him to get me out of the project, but then I just went back and reviewed what everybody had said. Okay, how do they talk about him? I had interviewed so many people, all the people who had known him—his mother, his father, his friends in school, and so on. He was a Goldwater delegate at the Republican convention. He was a Vietnam vet. He was a Catholic altar boy and on and on. Finally I began to understand that there was one common denominator: All the people I interviewed were angry with him; they felt betrayed. I asked myself, "What does that mean?" Because I am so literal-minded I went to my dictionary and looked up the word "betrayed." It has to do with a promise that is unfulfilled. I asked myself, "What is the promise he made?" He promised them that he was going to in some way or other fulfill them, make them whole, fulfill their ambitions for themselves. His was a hugely generous spirit. But in the end, of course, he was never able to do that for his wife or his children or his mother and father or the boy he had married, the boy who wanted to be a woman and for whom he was robbing the bank in order to get a sex change operation. Was that character grateful to him for it? He said, "Holy shit, I didn't ask him to rob a fucking bank, and now I am in trouble, jeez."

So Sonny also feels betrayed, and it was then that I understood the thematic underline of this character. He was somebody who wanted always to fulfill you. He was somebody who, when he walked up to you in the street and, in a sense, when he looked in your eyes, would be asking, "What is it that you want? I'll help you." You could ask him for anything, and he would do it. The problem was, he expected to get back love and reward and gratitude for doing these things, but he always failed—because none of us can ever bring other people's ideas and ambitions or aspirations to life. It's hard enough to do that for ourselves. So when he failed, what he got from them was a sense of betrayal.

From that time on, I knew what he would do in that bank. I also knew how to organize the plot—the sequence in which things would happen. Take, for example, the moment that he is trapped inside the bank. In fact, it was purely by chance that somebody across the street saw something that seemed a little odd about the bank. He called the police. The police came. Sonny and his hostages were trapped inside the bank. But I thought how much more interesting it would be to integrate that whole thing. The very thing that traps him in the bank is the same impulse that led him to go in in the first place. So there was a consistency throughout. At the last minute, the women hostages need to go to the bathroom and, of course, he obliges. It costs him time. A telephone call comes to the bank. It's the cops who have arrived outside and are set up across the street. If Sonny had not been willing to help those women go to the bathroom, he could have gotten away scot-free, but he was trapped in the bank for the very reason that he had gone there in the first place. So it all becomes one consistent narrative concept.

FROUG: A man trying to please everybody.

PIERSON: Exactly.

FROUG: Do you think great dialogue is vital to a picture?

PIERSON: The only thing that I think is vital to a picture is the sense of music and dance and structure. Everything else is wonderful: I mean, it's great to have good pictures. It's great to have good composition. It's great to have good costumes to tell the story. It's great to have good production design, and it's great to have a director who has the sense of rhythm and one thing or another to execute it. I think all of these details are extremely important, because genius is in the details. It's stupid to say that we don't care whether we have a good DP, because the images are important. That's not what I am saying, and I would not say that the dialogue is unimportant or that it doesn't matter whether the writer has an ear for the manner of speaking of the character about whom he or she is writing. Nonetheless, I think dialogue is only one of the aspects of film.

FROUG: What do you mean when you say "music and dance" in reference to film?

PIERSON: More and more, I think of film not as a visual medium so much as a musical medium. What you essentially are doing is telling stories with movement—the actions of bodies in space and time. And the time is the rhythm of the inner music of the characters involved. I often thought that if I were running a studio and looking for where I would recruit directors, I would look among choreographers, because that's what they do.

FROUG: Gene Kelly wasn't all that successful as a director.

"More and more, I think of film not as a visual medium so much as a musical medium. What you essentially are doing is telling stories with movement—the actions of bodies in space and time."

PIERSON: No, but he aligned himself with a man who also had a sense of dance and who also had a great visual sense, Stanley Donen. The two of them came together to become what I would rate one single great director, although Stanley Donen moved on to do other pictures which were far more successful than the pictures Gene Kelly directed.

Here's the thing: Film is the succession of still images, one after the other, twenty-four frames a second, and each frame adds more information to the one before it, and each adds very specific detailing in various kinds of ways. We get information from each frame, even though we are not thinking about that because the frames are moving too fast. This is the way it is built up; and I have an aesthetic built around that. In making a film, every single additional moment or second you are considering every single detail: What is in the corner of that frame? What does that picture on that wall say? What does the way the character's tie is tied or untied or loose or absent tell us about that character? We are getting those details twenty-four times every second. That is the basic underlying rhythm of film, from which you go on to extend to the idea that it is far more like music, because it is the shifting and changing of things in tempos and rhythms that is more important than anything else.

FROUG: You happen to be a world-class director, and I wonder now if you are not reinforcing the auteur theory?

PIERSON: No, no, no. Not at all. I am only saying that it's all a matter of considering those kinds of things an orchestra conductor or a choreographer, who are not necessarily the persons who have written the music, might consider. I have had problems with the auteur theory. The fact of the matter is that, between directing and writing, writing is incredibly more difficult at every single level.

Talking about music, in terms of writing, you could talk to students about a symphony, for example. The basic pattern for symphonies is the sonata form, in which you use one theme to express one thing, and then you bring in a second theme, contrapuntally or in a lot of different ways, to express something else. You have two themes, constantly in opposition, which you mix together and interpret. They dance with each other until there is a resolution, which may be a conquering of one by the other. What better way to think about doing a cop show? The cops are one theme of a sonata and the bad guys are the other, interweaving, contrapuntally manipulated. Or it's rondo form, in which you take a simple theme and repeat it over and over again. A film example of a rondo would be *Two for the Road*.

FROUG: It's going around in circles?

PIERSON: It is going around in circles, but it's developing as it goes around. To me, this is a far more interesting way of thinking about writing a screenplay than whether or not you have a crisis in the first fucking act on page seventeen.

FROUG: Do you think that the classic paradigm is bullshit?

PIERSON: Oh, I think it is. That's painting by the numbers. In general, people either have the physical facility for mixing the paints or they don't. Some people have an ear or they don't. It's almost like saying that either you can write or you can't write. That doesn't mean you can't learn to write, in the sense that you have to keep trying to do it and do it over and over again until it

"The fact of the matter is that, between directing and writing, writing is incredibly more difficult at every single level."

begins to come to you more and more naturally. But the really important thing about writing is how to think about writing, how to think about the characters that are in your piece—who they are and what it is they want.

Coming back to breaking it down into the most fractionated split seconds, one of the things I find extremely slovenly about most movies is that there is a startling lack of precision. If you look at a clown or somebody who is doing something very, very powerfully in an acting way, you see every single moment of it: They are angry. They look back. They go to the door or they don't. Everything is very specific. But what our young actors tend to do today, and the directors let them, is slip into an easy rhythm, so that nothing has any kind of specific meaning. So you can't single out, in the unconscious way that you need to, what is happening—you can't figure out what they are doing. Great acting is almost always so specific. Boy, oh boy, look at Marlon Brando, for example. He may appear to move at the pace of a turtle, but if you watch him doing it, everything he does is one single gesture after another and everything is very clear and simple.

FROUG: As a director, working with actors, did you focus on this specificity?

PIERSON: I had the joy of working mostly with actors whom I didn't have to teach how to act. That's not the job of the director. If you've got an actor who needs to learn how to act, the best thing to do is replace him.

I think that it is obligatory for a director to create an atmosphere on the set in which all of the actors know that they are safe and are not going to be allowed to make fools of themselves. Then they can begin to experiment and begin to play. One of the things that has gone out of this film business is a sense of playfulness. There is increasingly this kind of heaviness, this weight of making the day's schedule and this fear of somebody making a mistake. If somebody says something in rehearsal and the producer on the set charges in and says, "Holy shit, he is not going to do it that way, is he?" the director needs to be strong enough to pick up the producer, throw him off the set, and say, "Come back later and we'll show you. And then you talk to me about it; don't say it in front of the actors."

FROUG: Do you have problems getting actors to understand specificity?

PIERSON: There is a tendency, and it's a very strong one, for all of the actors to fall into the rhythms of the strongest personality on the set. So all of a sudden they all begin to walk and talk in the same kind of rhythm. You need to break that up. You have to go over and say something. For example, I tell them that every time another actor keeps pushing you, if he comes right in on top of you, throw him for a loop. If you say your line and he comes right in on top of your line, why don't you wait a little while and look in his eyes before you speak.

FROUG: That's a sure way to make your point, I imagine. Do you plan to direct more?

PIERSON: Oh God, I don't know. It's such a physical grind, and I don't enjoy it for the sake of directing itself. The things that I would like to direct are those screenplays that I see with such a clarity and specificity and depth of feeling that I know what I want to do with them. In those circumstances, directing is a great joy, provided you can get the facilities and the support. But just to take a job in order to be a director is, to me, simply not worth it. Thank God, after *A Star Is Born* became a huge hit, my percentage of net profit paid off. I never have to work again unless I want to.

FROUG: *A Star Is Born* wasn't a total pleasure, was it?

PIERSON: Well, there was a lot of bad press about the making of the picture while it was going on: the fights between Barbra and me, Barbra and Jon, and Jon Peters and myself. The fact of the matter is that over the seventy-two or seventy-five days or whatever the hell it took to make it, on four out of five days, and all five days in some weeks, we were fine. It was on the sixth or seventh day or whatever that we would have really, really, really, really rough battles because everybody cared so much. The point is that when I look back on it, I remember more fun. In fact, Barbra and I have talked about this. She said, "The only time I got upset was when you weren't doing it right."

FROUG: That's a funny line. I know you say dialogue is not critical, but you really made an impact on the language with a line in *Cool Hand Luke*: "What we have here is a failure to communicate." Did you imagine, when you wrote that line, that it was going to resonate as it did, become part of the language?

PIERSON: No. I can still remember very vividly the moment when I wrote it: I was sitting in my study overlooking the ocean in Malibu, and those words popped out onto the paper—in those days I typed on an Underwood. I looked at them and thought, "Shit, that's pretty good." And then I thought, "Oh God, everybody's going to ask how this dumb prison guard can say that: This redneck guy wouldn't talk like that. It's not the right language." So I wrote a whole little biography about what happens in the Florida prison systems, and it had nothing to do with anything in reality. I made up that, to get promoted from a prison guard to a camp commander, you had to take courses in criminology and penology and one thing and another at the University of Miami, so he became acquainted with this slightly sophisticated language in that way. The fact of the matter is, nobody ever questioned it. I never had to produce the biography to justify it.

FROUG: How long did you spend writing that classic?

PIERSON: From the time I started writing it until the picture was done, I would say probably about a year and a half. But my first draft was 205 pages because, to bring myself to understand how Luke got to where he was when he was arrested, I started with him getting up in the morning, having a fight with his mother and his wife, leaving the house in anger, going out, playing pool, and other things: He went to church; no satisfaction there. Finally he gets in another fight and then winds up drunk, flipping off the tops of parking meters. That took about thirty pages, but I needed to write that for myself in order to help myself get a grasp of the character. Since then I've adopted that as a systematic method of exploring a character, especially a lead character. It's roughly the equivalent of what I regard as the proper use of improvisation à la the Stanislavsky method. It's a wonderful way to get inside a character.

FROUG: Writing various, almost random scenes until you get inside the character?

PIERSON: When I reach a point where I have a scene that I can't make work, I try not to spend any time just sitting there and staring into space, because not much is going to happen, at least with me. So I try to be active about it and say, "All right, something is wrong with this scene. I can't figure out what's wrong. I know what the scene is suppose to do in the structure of the story, but the characters can't make it work. So something is wrong with the characters coming into it. They don't have the right attitude or whatever it is that is going to generate this scene." Maybe I don't know the characters well enough, so I just explore them. Is it a husband and wife sitting down to talk about something or other or to do something together? They are about to go to a party, but right away they get into an argument in the car? Well, why did they get into an argument in the car? What happened to them last night or this morning that could explain this? So I begin to write those scenes and just play around with things. I put the characters in situations: For example, how would he change a tire on the freeway during rush hour? Would he be like Warren Beatty? Does he pull right over in the fast lane and take off his shirt and start to change the tire? Or would he bump along and ruin a perfectly good tire until he gets to a safe off-ramp where he could go and take it to a Unocal station and get it changed? That's one way I get into a character.

Unless I can understand why the characters do what they do, the scene won't work. Otherwise, if you do the scene, you just write the plot. That's all it's going to be, a recitation. Somebody said this; somebody said that; and then the next thing happens. It's a plot.

"Unless I can understand why the characters do what they do, the scene won't work."

FROUG: So, you need to know everybody's attitude in a scene, right?

PIERSON: In detail.

FROUG: Would you want to elaborate on that?

PIERSON: Yeah. I mean, that would simply come naturally to you, as with the character in *Dog Day*: Once I had figured out that essential aspect of him, I knew intuitively how he would act. I didn't have to think. You could ask me what the character would do if he was ordering dinner at Spago or what he would do if . . . whatever.

FROUG: You are presently working on a screenplay. Can you talk about that? It's for Disney, right?

PIERSON: Yeah, but that's probably dead right now. That's a Michael Crichton story which was very interesting because Michael's stories are intricate and technical and very well worked out in terms of plot. That's not normally how I approach things, so it was a very interesting meeting of minds, and we had some fun together. But unfortunately, I think it's probably going to be set aside. It's too expensive a film for Disney to make at this time.

FROUG: What have these sixty-to-eighty-million-dollar budgets done to the film writer?

PIERSON: They have brought in an enormous number of people with variant points of view. This is not to fault them; their jobs are to make money for the studio in whatever way they are employed to do so. But they are not people who are thinking about the story in terms of themes and character and music and dance and play and fun or playability. Very few of them have ever had any experience in the theater or working with actors or directors. More and more of them are MBAs from Harvard Business School, which I think is a communist plot. In any case, they are thinking about the story in completely different ways. You've got eight people in a room. One of them is wondering if there is a toy that we can invent. Another is wondering if it is going to offend some segment of the audience. Another is saying, "We've got to have a big star, and the star we want is . . ." And they list a whole bunch of people who are utterly inappropriate for the story.

FROUG: One of them is probably asking, "What kind of new explosions can we get in it?"

PIERSON: The directors do that. My God, I don't do those kinds of pictures.

FROUG: You don't write those kinds of pictures?

PIERSON: Well, I have done it. There is a picture around right now that is something I did for Universal some years ago. It has come alive again; they are considering doing it. It has some huge action sequences and explosions. Not all of which have much relevance to the theme of what the picture is about.

I turned down the first Rambo picture. It was offered to me to write, but I thought, thematically, it was just not something that I could do and feel honest with myself. If you are raising the issue of violence in films, I think it's a matter of individual conscience. I don't see how we can delegate the issue of censoring films to any organization of any kind. Consider the serious films that I have done: One winds up with Paul Newman being shot deliberately right through the throat, executed by a guard at

prison, and another has Al Pacino's friend being shot right
through the middle of the head. Should I not have made these
pictures?

FROUG: Those are individual actions that are part and parcel of
the characters and the stories. They are not gratuitous, as in,
"How we can get a car chase in here?"

PIERSON: Well, I'll give you an example from the picture that I am
considering doing right now, which I don't want to talk about
for the obvious reasons. There is a moment when there is a great
shootout, and into the middle of it wanders a thirteen-year-old
girl, a dope addict, who just happens to be trapped there, and
one of the dope dealers blows her away with a double-barreled
shotgun. I said, "I'll do the picture on one condition, which is
that you not do that because it is unforgivable. I will not lend my
name to it."

FROUG: It had nothing to do with the story?

PIERSON: It had nothing to do with the story. No reason for it. I
don't know why it's there.

FROUG: Why is it there? Let's talk about that. Why do the studios
feel this need to bring in a thirteen-year-old girl and blast her to
pieces?

PIERSON: Bill, listen, I don't think it's just the studios. That's the
worst part of it. I think it's the directors. I think it is the writers
themselves who have become so desensitized to this that they
believe that those are the kinds of things that sell films, that sell
certain kinds of audiences that they want to appeal to. I think that
what the creative community has done to itself is one of the most

destructive trends in the last few years. As films have become so expensive, the decisions to go ahead with them are weighted with such financial consequences for the people who make those commitments. So more and more emphasis is being put on getting that audience of fourteen-to-eighteen-year-old boys, because they are the ones who come to films, and they are the ones who see them over and over again. That is what is happening with the writers and, to a lesser extent, with the directors.

You have an idea for something that you think will make a great film. But you look at what they are interested in doing and you say, "What is the point in trying to put myself through developing a treatment? What is the point in getting myself up to go and make a pitch and sell this idea, or write an original, which is a huge investment of time and energy? Why should I do that when I know that the chances of selling it and of ever seeing it made are less and less and less than they have ever been?" I think that leads to self-censorship, which I think is terribly, terribly sad. But it is happening all over Hollywood.

"Everything is 'mallized,' everything is 'Wal-Martized,' and everything is a matter of merchandising."

FROUG: We seem to be in the process of "dumbing-down" America. It seems that everything is made for this fourteen-year-old boy or girl who goes to see a movie again and again. What is the reason for this situation?

PIERSON: It's just part of the market economy. The same thing is happening to our towns and our cities. Everything is "mallized," everything is "Wal-Martized," and everything is a matter of merchandising. For example, it becomes increasingly difficult to get really good and fresh food to cook, of individual quality, because everything is being manufactured consistently to one single standard.

FROUG: To the mass market.

PIERSON: To the mass market. So the movies are only one aspect
of what is happening in the larger society. I don't think that
many people understand that one of the problems of the movie
business here is that the choking point is the distribution
system. You can make good independent films, but how do you
get them out there to the people who might want to see them?
You can't, because the distribution system has become so
exclusively devoted to distributing this mass-market material.
The same thing is happening in our supermarkets. The way
they have positioned themselves is that the one place where
you can go and easily get food, they don't sell food anymore—
they sell shelf space to wholesalers who come in and control
their shelf space. So if you make a specialized product that
happens to have a great value, like an independent filmmaker
who tries to go out and sell an independent film to the dis-
tributors, you've got to go to a supermarket to rent shelf space.
And you know who is up there against you? Coca-Cola and
Pepsi-Cola and Beatrice. And they just grab you off the shelf.
So where are you going to sell your product?

FROUG: Let's go back to the screenwriter sitting at home. He's
written three or four scripts. He's getting better, we hope, and
now he wants to break into this fortress called Hollywood. How
does he do that?

PIERSON: Well, I don't know. One thing I do know is that the pros
who do this kind of shit are very, very good at it. So there's not
much point in trying to compete with them unless you have a lot
of history or just happen to be extraordinarily precocious. So why

try to? The best thing to do is write the best script that you care about in the deepest kind of way. The important thing to you is to get your foot into the door and get an opportunity to do something on the same basis that somebody in the business has. So you give it to me and I pass it to somebody who gets it to an agent. The agent calls some person who hands the script to the studio and says, "Look, you're not going to make this screenplay and nobody else is going to make it, but this kid can write."

I am not even sure that if I were to start over again that I would want to get into this business now. I think I might rather become a playwright, or try to become a playwright, although I've tried and I've discovered that I don't have it, or I haven't tried enough to find out. My instincts are so cinematic that I find myself totally lost; everything I write turns into a movie rather than a play. Maybe I would become a tugboat captain or something. That's a bunch of bullshit; I wouldn't want to do that.

FROUG: What was your toughest job? And why was it so tough?

PIERSON: The toughest ones were for the pictures that did not work, and I could not find a way to make work. Some of them were made, and some, thank God, were not made.

They're all tough. The difficulty is in the nature of the first draft. What you have done in the course of creating the first draft is bring order out of chaos. Up to that point, you have no idea; you're fighting desperation; you're so sad. Suddenly you find a way to make sense of it all and to get it down on paper. The first time you do it, it's like a sketch, and you have to think of it as a sketch: Now I can see the design in this thing. Now I can begin to apply a little color and maybe expand that line and pull it in

"What you have done in the course of creating the first draft is bring order out of chaos."

here and do all that. Then I get to another level, and I suddenly stop and look at it. Dustin Hoffman talks about this a lot. He said that you get something to a point that you think is just wonderful, and then you say, "Oh, I know what this picture is going to be, and it's going to be so exciting." Then you read it the next day and realize that it's shit. Well, that's Dustin, and his particular problem is that he sees it as shit. I do not. What I see when I read it the next day are glimmers of another level that I can go to. But in order to do that, I will have to tear apart what I have already created, which is something that I care deeply about. I mean, what is a story but a matter of subduing our most chaotic terrors—the kinds of things that psychoanalysis was only invented to nibble at—and reducing them to something that is bearable and understandable? And if I understand it, then I can write it. We're talking about the idea of moving from draft to draft. At each level that you reach, you have to tear up what you have done before, which cost an enormous amount of psychological and emotional energy. That makes the process of rewriting very, very difficult. And I don't know any screenplay that I have ever worked on where I did not go through ten to twelve or sometimes sixteen drafts before I showed it to anybody. You just need to do that. You need to keep recycling it and refining it until you finally get to the point where you can't think about it anymore. I don't think anything is ever finished, but there comes a day when you have to walk away from it. Otherwise you wind up doing the same damned thing forever. You're like Camus' character who had been writing a novel for forty years and never got beyond rewriting the first sentence.

FROUG: Do you begin to rewrite before you finish a draft, or do you finish a draft and then go back and rewrite?

PIERSON: That varies. A lot depends on the circumstances and the situation. If you have a plot, it helps an enormous amount, because you forge through, knowing that there are scenes that are missing, which you kind of skip over. I really try to write straight through. Then go back.

FROUG: Let it sit for a while to get a perspective on it?

PIERSON: Yeah. And all of us have a few close friends whom we will give it to and say, "What do you think?" You know what happens? If, at lunch, I give it to Alvin Sargent, who is one of the writers who does this for me, by the time I have driven back home, I am already on the phone to say, "Alvin, listen, you don't need to read it, because I am free from it." The mere fact of giving it to somebody, and that somebody else is actually reading it, frees you up to begin to go to the next level.

FROUG: Do you then wait for the feedback, or do you just go back and start reworking it?

PIERSON: I'll start reworking it. Then I'll get the feedback and I'll rework it some more. And then there comes a day when you say, "Okay, I have got to get out of the house."

FROUG: Do you ever wait somewhat trembling for a response from a buyer? Do you still get nervous?

PIERSON: Yeah, yeah. Listen, you want to know whether your brains are still functioning, whether your heart is still there, but at the same time there are those things that you know in your heart of hearts are not okay. I did something for Ron Howard last year where we were having such fun with the screenplay all the way through, but I never got it to work. I knew that it didn't work, and I finally said to Ron, "I think this needs one of two things. It either needs a new writer with a new approach or it needs a radically different concept, because what we have now, even though there is so much of it that is so rich and works so well, really doesn't work." We agreed on that.

FROUG: It wasn't good enough?

PIERSON: "Not good enough" implies that somehow or other it's written in a slovenly manner or a cliché manner. No, I just could not make a connection to the central character so that I was able to explain him, to launch him on his journey through this project. The interesting thing was that everybody else on the project thought the problems were in the second and third act. I didn't think the problems were there. I thought the problems were with the first act, because if I could get the first act to work so that we knew what this man was after, then the whole thing would work. But I could not make it work. I never found that scene.

FROUG: I have a chapter in this book about the overemphasis on the need to have a rooting interest in the protagonist. Do you agree?

PIERSON: Yeah. Well, that is the casual phrase for what I am talking about, but I try to be more precise about it. It's a matter of truly having an emotional connection to the characters.

FROUG: I can't imagine a more despicable character than Roy Cohn. You won an Ace Award for *Citizen Cohn*. Tell me about having an emotional connection with this ruthless, dishonest, despicable son of a bitch.

PIERSON: Partly, it had to do with Jimmy Woods' performance. He understood what he was doing. He is extremely intelligent, and he's a very, very skilled actor. But Loring Mandel, who did a great deal of the rewrite on that project, really made it work.

Cohn was always testing the limits of how far he could go: At what point would people say, "No, you can't go any further"? He never reached those limits, which led him to become more and more contemptuous of everybody—hating them for what they were allowing him to do, which was whatever he damn well pleased. So on some subliminal level, I think that we were absorbed by that. We saw a man making a desperate cry for help, and finally, as he's beginning to die, he has an ending monologue in which he is asked by these imaginary creatures how he could have done the terrible things he did. In essence, he said, "I did this. I did that. I fucked everybody. I destroyed everybody's lives, and none of you ever stopped me." In essence, he said, "It wasn't my fault; you let it happen." Now, that is thematically and morally a very powerful theme about human existence. It has to do with the Holocaust.

FROUG: Blaming somebody else?

PIERSON: Not only blaming somebody else. I am talking about the audience's ability to identify. There is something else, too, and that is the acting out of the audience's nastiest impulses. We have all these impulses to be rude to other people, and many of the people that he was shoving around were not the best people.

FROUG: The fact that he was gay was his most horrible secret, right? Except that everybody knew it.

PIERSON: Everybody knew it, but in those days, nobody ever discussed those things. That was really an interesting aspect of it. By the way, we had an alternative ending. You know what the AIDS quilt is? Well, there are five patches in the AIDS quilt that are dedicated to Roy Cohn. With love and affection and what-not. And we got that section of the AIDS rug sent to us in Pittsburgh, where we were shooting. We photographed those particular ones as kind of a montage, and we did an ending in which we made note of that terrific irony of his life. What was so interesting was that the gay community in San Francisco, who was instrumental in getting this, were thrilled by it and thought that it was so interesting and such a great irony and all the rest of it. Then, when I showed it to an audience at Sundance, the New York people, especially, in the theater were enraged: One of them threatened to kill me if I used the ending.

In the end, I cut it out. This was a very powerful idea, a powerful irony and statement. But it was something that came a bit out of left field and took us in a different direction and made the picture about something else. In the end, I was more than pleased to have given up that ending, even though I loved the way it looked and the way it played. But it was off the point and made it about something that was not correct.

FROUG: If you had your extraordinary career to do over again, what would you do differently?

PIERSON: Somebody asked that of Woody Allen once. He said, "On the whole, I think I'd do pretty much everything the same, except maybe I would not go see *The Magus*."

*"I am not sure
that there are
certain things in
my personal life
that I would
change, that
I regret."*

I am not sure that there are certain things in my personal life that I would change, that I regret. As far as what I tried to do with my writing, I think that I exhausted my possibilities as much as I possibly could in every stage, and I could not have done any more. I've wished that I were brighter. I've wished that I were better educated. I've wished that I had more original ideas. I've wished that sometimes I had more courage. But at each point in my life, I think I pushed myself as hard as I could in all those categories. At least it has left me with no regrets, because I pushed myself as hard as I could.

FILMOGRAPHY

Writer

1965   *Cat Ballou* (shared credit), Academy Award nomination

1966   *The Happening* (shared credit)

1967   *Cool Hand Luke*, based on the novel by Donn Pearce, Academy Award nomination

1968   *The Looking Glass War*, based on the novel by John LeCarré

1969   *The Anderson Tapes*, based on the novel by Lawrence Sanders

1970   *Dog Day Afternoon*, Academy Award for Best Original Screenplay

1971   *A Star Is Born* (shared credit)

1978   *King of the Gypsies*, based on the book by Peter Maas

1980   *Haywire*

1981   *In Country* (shared credit), based on the novel by Bobbie
        AnnMason

1982   *Presumed Innocent* (shared credit), based on the novel by
        Scott Turow

Director

1970   *The Neon Ceiling*, television movie

1971   *The Looking Glass War*

1972   *A Star Is Born*

1973   *King of the Gypsies*

1974   *Somebody Has to Shoot the Picture*, television movie, Cable
        ACE Award for Best Direction

1975   *Citizen Cohn*, television movie, Cable ACE Award for
        Best Direction

1994   *Lakota Woman: Siege at Wounded Knee*, television movie

1995   *Truman*, television movie

Catching the Big One

An Interview with

Brian Helgeland

"I am cynical about a lot of things, but I am not cynical about the fact that if you have talent, someone will figure it out, because there is too much hunger for it out there."

— Brian Helgeland

A big, ambling, comfortable-looking man with tufts of brown hair sticking out from under his soft felt hat entered the room wearing shorts, a khaki shirt, and a big, shy smile. He was the screenwriter who had burst onto America's screens with his Oscar-winning screenplay for *L.A. Confidential*, based on James Ellroy's exciting novel that was so overloaded with plot and character complexities that most Hollywood writers considered it impossible to turn it into a coherent movie. The novel was talked about, but, like the weather, nobody could do anything about it—until Brian Helgeland came along. This kid, this commercial fisherman who had won an obscure screenwriting contest, did what the seasoned pros couldn't. We all applauded him.

Helgeland was not, however, content to sit back, rest on his achievement, and wait for somebody to come to him to adapt a book or rewrite a "needs work" screenplay. He immediately went to work creating his own original stories and screenplays. To no one's surprise, he sold them and became one of the most sought-after young screenwriters in Hollywood. In a rare instance of a studio knowing what it's doing, Warner Bros. took Helgeland under its corporate wing and began to recommend him to producers and directors. Thus he came to the attention of Richard Donner. And thanks to Donner, Helgeland came ambling into the director's guesthouse, where I was ensconced for the nine days, conducting interviews for this book.

FROUG: Dick Donner says you're a kid from a fishing village, true?

HELGELAND: Yeah, well, I'm Norwegian-American. I'm from New Bedford, Massachusetts, which is a big commercial fishing town. It was a big whaling town. That's the town where Father Mapple makes a speech from the pulpit in the beginning of *Moby-Dick*.

FROUG: How did you get from there to screenwriting?

HELGELAND: When I was in college, I was an English major. When I graduated, I couldn't get a job. I didn't know what I wanted to do. I always loved movies, but it had never occurred to me that people could make a living writing movies. My dad had been a commercial fisherman when I was a kid, and I became a commercial fisherman for almost two years. My second winter was coming up, and I didn't want to go fishing for the winter. I had some money saved up, and I was thinking of going to Florida or someplace warm for the winter. But in a bookstore I saw a book about film schools, which I didn't even know existed. I applied, and the only one I could get into in mid-semester was a school in Los Angeles called Loyola. I got into film school to stay warm. There I took a class in screenwriting, which was just a requirement for the course. I took that class with no intentions of writing, and wrote a script that ended up winning a student film award.

FROUG: What was the script called?

HELGELAND: It was called *McAfee's War*.

FROUG: Did it get made?

HELGELAND: No, it never got made.

FROUG: How did you get the assignment to write *L.A. Confidential*? Most people understood that that book couldn't be made into a movie, and yet you won an Oscar for it. Tell me how you did that.

HELGELAND: I don't know. I wish I did, so I could do it again. I'm a big fan of Ellroy. He is the only author I ever stood in line to have a book signed by. When I heard that Warner had bought the rights to *L.A. Confidential*, I began a nine-month lobbying effort to get hired to do it.

FROUG: How did you go about doing that?

HELGELAND: I just kept trying to get a meeting, basically to tell everyone how I would do it and that I had worked at Warner.

FROUG: What did you do at Warner?

HELGELAND: I had done a Viking movie for them and had sold them a spec Sherlock Holmes script called *Elementary*.

FROUG: You told me you had to campaign to get the job. How did you do it?

HELGELAND: Warner had bought it to make a David Wolper miniseries out of it. They couldn't get that going. I think there was no way that they could make it for television. They needed to water it down, to clean it up enough to make a television miniseries out of it. So it just hung around for a while. And I kept trying to get in for a meeting and to talk to the different executives that were involved. Finally I spoke to Billy Gerber, who was the executive on it, and he put me in touch with Curtis Hanson, who had just been hired to direct it. I met Hanson and convinced him to let me get going on it while he was off finishing up *The River Wild*. That was the beginning of this long process of three or four years before it got made.

FROUG: How long did it take you to write it?

HELGELAND: The first draft took about three or four months.

FROUG: It's a terribly complex book. How did you come up with a spine, an action line?

HELGELAND: The thing about the book was that I loved it. But it was very complicated—it had ten different plots going on. It had these three characters of Bud White, Ed Exley, and Jack Vincennes, who were very strong characters who went all the way through the book. Despite how complicated the novel was and how dense the plot, these three main characters stood out very strongly. The first thing Curtis and I decided to do was to was throw out every scene that didn't have any one of those three characters in it, which cut the book down about a quarter. Then I just tried to get to the essence of those three characters and to get rid of everything that didn't apply, keeping the things that did, reworking some of them. I wrote some scenes to break certain things and condense and combine certain elements. Using that as a template for working on the movie, the screenplay got to where it had a strong line.

FROUG: How the hell you did this, I still don't know. And after that you wrote *Conspiracy Theory*?

HELGELAND: Yes, but *L.A. Confidential* became a process of lots of revisions and long waits to try to get the movie made. When Curtis was done with *The River Wild*, we worked together and just kept going, although there was not a lot of interest from the studio in making the movie really. I think the studio just didn't quite know what to do with it. *Mulholland Falls* was out at the time, and they were leery about bringing out the second L.A. period movie of the year. In the end, it got put into turnaround, and New Regency, Arnon Milchan and David Matalon, picked it up. We had a reading for them. We brought in a bunch of actors and read through the script once, and Arnon said, "It's great. Let's make it." The next thing we knew we were casting it.

FROUG: Were you involved after that?

HELGELAND: We had four weeks of rehearsals before we started shooting with the actors, which was great—it made for a very uncomplicated set because all the concerns of the actors were dealt with ahead of time.

FROUG: Were you still revising the screenplay?

HELGELAND: Oh, yeah. We revised for the actors, and almost until the night the movie came out, we were still revising. The voice-over of Danny DeVito, especially his opening narration, was always under revision.

FROUG: Were you surprised by the Oscar?

HELGELAND: It's a terrible thing to say, but by the time the Oscars came around, I fully expected to win, only because the screenplay had won so many things leading up to it and, dumb as it sounds, the odds in Las Vegas were overwhelming. They were even money for me to win the best screenplay, so I was very strangely confident we would win.

FROUG: Did it affect your career?

HELGELAND: It didn't really, in that I wanted to direct and I had already directed a film leading up to the Oscars, so winning for screenwriting didn't really affect my directing. In a way, it left my writing career the same. As far as being a writer for hire or a writer for other directors it had no impact. I left that behind me, so it didn't really affect me. Even though it might have made me more attractive, I wasn't taking those jobs anymore. So, in a weird sort of way, it didn't affect my career.

FROUG: What was your next writing venture?

HELGELAND: In chronological writing time, *Conspiracy Theory*.

FROUG: That was an original, wasn't it?

HELGELAND: Yeah, that was an original. After I did a couple of drafts of *L.A. Confidential*, I started writing *Conspiracy Theory*.

FROUG: Tell me about writing it.

HELGELAND: I was working on two different ideas: One was a street thriller about a New York cabdriver who was paranoid and published a newsletter, and the other story was a love story about two people who couldn't be together. I couldn't lick either one of the stories. The love story problem was I couldn't think of a reason why people in 1996, or whatever year it was at the time, couldn't be together. It seemed like all those barriers of race, religion, etc. could be overcome. Then it dawned on me one day: You couldn't be with someone if they were insane. So I got my insane cabdriver from my other project and stuck him in my love story, and it all fell together after that.

FROUG: It did indeed. So how did that affect you?

HELGELAND: I don't really know. It affected me as a writer in that the film was directed by Richard Donner, and he and I got along really well. He had me on the set for the entire shoot.

FROUG: That's rare, isn't it?

HELGELAND: Yeah. I could see how a lot of writers gripe about changes that get made, because a lot of times writers work in a vacuum—they are not in that sort of "real" world, the process that the filmmakers are actually involved in. It was very valuable to me to see the different problems that could arise.

FROUG: Great training for a guy who wants to be a director?

HELGELAND: Yeah, as far as that goes. I would sit behind the director and play this game where I tried to guess what lens was on based on what the image on the monitor looked like, compared to how far away the camera was from the actors. And Donner would also point out different things to me. It also helped as far as hearing the actors. Lots of times, dialogue that seemed to sound good to you in your head when you were writing it made you want to crawl under a rock when the actors said it.

FROUG: Does it help, as you are writing, to speak all the lines out loud?

HELGELAND: Yeah. I usually do that.

FROUG: Sort of play the scenes to yourself?

HELGELAND: Yeah. Weirdly enough, on *L.A. Confidential*, we had Russell Crowe and Guy Pearce, Australian actors, playing Americans. And they have a certain difficulty with some of their "r"s, so that became a screenwriting problem. Sometimes I had to phrase something a different way so they wouldn't give away the fact that they were Australian, which they never did. It's interesting, the things that happen on the set that you have to deal with as a writer as compared with the things that happen in your cubbyhole while you're working away.

FROUG: When working on a screenplay, do you use a paradigm? Do you say you have to be on such and such a page for a climax?

HELGELAND: Yeah. Generally I work in three acts, but, I think, in a very natural way. Life is three acts, so it seems like a very natural form. I'm not conscious of it; I don't worry about it. I am not a slave to what has to be on page thirty or page ninety or whatever. But you need those gearshifts in there or it's not interesting. I am a big believer in outlining, because I think a lot of good screenwriting is in having good structure.

FROUG: How long do you spend on outlining?

HELGELAND: I probably spend a little over half my time writing a script outlining it.

FROUG: How long before you start writing the screenplay? A couple of months?

HELGELAND: Yeah, roughly. I'd say about four months altogether. Lots of times I'll have an idea, but I can't just sit down and write an idea when I have it because I have to think about it. As odd as it sounds, when I come up with an idea for an original that I know I am going to write, my eyes water. I usually spend three or four days just trying to figure out what the idea is or who the character is. And then I leave it alone. I won't work on it for six months or a year, but somewhere in the back of the head it

"Generally I work in three acts, but, I think, in a very natural way. Life is three acts, so it seems like a very natural form."

percolates and, all of a sudden, one day it's time to work on it, so I start working on it.

FROUG: When you finally start to work on it, do you just stay with it?

HELGELAND: When I start, I focus on that one thing and that's all I do.

FROUG: What drives you? The characters?

HELGELAND: Yeah. I am very interested in the characters. I first think they are one thing, and then they figure out they are something else. Characters don't quite know who they are at the beginning, whether they think they do or not. They learn about themselves over the course of the film.

FROUG: As we chatted earlier, you said that *Cool Hand Luke* was the movie that kicked you off as a screenwriter. I'm interested in what starts writers on the road to becoming screenwriters.

HELGELAND: I don't know how old I was when I first saw *Cool Hand Luke*. I guess about ten. I saw it on television. That movie has always stuck with me. It's a very subjective, personal thing, but, by my definition, it's the best film ever made and certainly the best film ever written, although I think it's very well directed too. I am so attracted to that character—that loner—that I can watch it anytime. He's just such a quintessential movie character for me. It shows you how big a movie can be when it is just dealing with the people and really nothing else. I own *Cool Hand Luke* in every conceivable format, and I am proud to say that I've seen it projected five times.

FROUG: You started by writing spec screenplays. Do you think that this is the best way for writers to get started?

HELGELAND: I personally don't know any other way. I think the only way to get a break as a writer is to write something that you can show to people. Because in Hollywood everything is based on what you've done. If you've done nothing as far as having a film produced, you at least have a script to show that you can write.

FROUG: Did you write many scripts before you had one that you were able to show?

HELGELAND: Yeah. Actually, the very first script I wrote won an award, so I thought I knew everything. After that, the next seven were almost unreadable. Whatever I knew on that first one, I'd forgotten already and I had to relearn. Before I got adept at it, I had to write about ten scripts.

FROUG: Is it tough to get into the business now? Are they reading scripts?

HELGELAND: I don't know. I didn't know who read scripts when I was breaking in, and I don't know who reads them now. But someone reads them. I am cynical about a lot of things, but I am not cynical about the fact that if you have talent, someone will figure it out, because there is too much hunger for it out there.

FROUG: If you have talent, you will get there?

HELGELAND: I really think so. You also have to have perseverance. In a lot of ways, screenwriting is sort of the last-man-standing kind of thing. The last man standing sells the script or makes a career out of it. So many people are more than willing to dismiss you, so you have to be your own champion. Who else do you expect to do it?

FROUG: How do you get them to read a script?

HELGELAND: I think you really have to get an agent first. It's a classic catch-22.

FROUG: Did you get an agent first?

HELGELAND   I did, yeah.

FROUG: By sending him these spec scripts?

HELGELAND: In my case, because of the film school contest, I got an agent. That little bleep of recognition alerted someone to the idea that maybe there was something there.

FROUG: There's a guy who could write.

HELGELAND: Yeah. Personally, that's the only way I know how to get an agent. Generally, I would say you have to be in Los Angeles. There are no two ways about it. You can't do it over the phone or through the mail. You actually have to be here. L.A. is full of people trying to break into the film business one way or the other. What I have seen is that they become their own little community, and when one of them breaks in, that person becomes a conduit for all his friends.

FROUG: So networking is important?

HELGELAND: I think it is crucial. That person that you met some-where or other—even at the beach—who is an assistant at an agency can get your script into that agency and get it read. There are a million ways in, but you have to start from the back door and from underneath. You can't just call some big literary agent and expect that he is going to call you back and want to read your script.

FROUG: Did you get a big literary agent or a small one?

HELGELAND: Very small.

   FROUG: Those seem to be the hungry guys who are looking for new writers.

HELGELAND: Yeah, yeah. Writers come and go and move on to bigger agencies, so the smaller agents are looking for young writers. I don't think I really ever met anyone who had genuine talent who didn't succeed at some level. I have met a lot of people with very marginal talent who, just because they kept at it so much, have made a niche for themselves. With all the new cable and 190 channels and foreign and syndicated whatever, plus television shows and low-budget movies, there is such a demand for product and scripts. I really think that if you stick at it long enough, you will be successful.

   FROUG: Donner is very excited about a new original screenplay by you. Do you want to talk a little about it?

HELGELAND: Yeah, sure. I don't know what it's going to be called eventually, but right now it's called *The High Lonesome*. It's a movie about the Civil War, a Western about a young Union soldier at Gettysburg who is deafened by a cannon blast. He's from Boston, and when he tries to go back home, he realizes that he doesn't fit in anymore. So he decides to go west and seek his fortune. Basically, because of everything that happens to him, he becomes a gunfighter. He's a deaf gunfighter in the Old West. The story is really just about a guy who loses his humanity to some extent and has to try to find a way to get it back.

   FROUG: What appeals to you, a former commercial fisherman, about the West?

HELGELAND: Well, in this case, it's actually an idea that Dick has had for a long time. He wanted to do a movie about a deaf gunfighter. On the set of *Conspiracy Theory*, we got to talking about it. He told me about this odd little guy who was running around out West. I became enamored with the character, and Dick asked me if I could try to come up with a screenplay for it. I just finished it.

FROUG: Why is the seemingly old-fashioned Western genre of any interest to you young guys? Is this era still really vital? Does it have life?

HELGELAND: Yeah. I think the classic Western is a character study. I think that in the last decade or so people forgot that the Western is about character. They tried to come up with some high-concept Westerns that really didn't work. For me, the best Westerns are all just character pieces. If it's well done, a Western can be just as viable today as anytime, because you are really just telling a story of a person. If it is compelling enough, it should translate to any time or place.

FROUG: What is your favorite genre?

HELGELAND: I really don't have one. I just love movies where people are put into extreme circumstances and you see which way they zig or zag, like in *Cool Hand Luke*, with this loner, this rebel being stuck in prison. Another film I really like a lot is *Deliverance*, where you have four guys on a joyride wind up in a life-or-death situation. Just to see what happens with those characters when they get stuck in that crucible makes for a great story.

"I think the classic Western is a character study. I think that in the last decade or so people forgot that the Western is about character."

[114]

FROUG: Dramatic tension is built in?

HELGELAND: Yeah. Whatever the genre is, that's what you need.

FROUG: How would you like to wrap this up?

HELGELAND: It's good to be a little bit miserable. I don't think happy people make the best screenwriters. I think that if you can find a way to get a little misery into your life, you can find a way to use that misery and write about it, and it will be a huge help to you.

"I just love movies where people are put into extreme circumstances and you see which way they zig or zag. . . ."

FILMOGRAPHY

1988	*976-EVIL* (shared credit)
1989	*A Nightmare on Elm Street 4* (shared credit)
1990	*Highway to Hell*
1995	*Assassins* (shared credit)
1997	*L.A. Confidential*, Academy Award, Best Adaptation
1997	*Conspiracy Theory*
1997	*The Postman* (shared credit)
1999	*Payback* (shared credit), also directed

"I don't know exactly what I'm going to write until I actually sit down and write."
— Joe Eszterhas, *The New Screenwriter Looks at the New Screenwriter*

"I do my plotting in my head as I go along, and usually I do it wrong and have to do it all over again. I know there are writers who plot their stories in great detail before they begin to write them, but I am not one of that group. With me plots are not made; they grow. And if they refuse to grow, you throw the stuff away and start over again."
— Raymond Chandler, *Raymond Chandler Speaking*

"I work under the same rules that a spy master works with his agents. They have a rule called 'Need to Know.' You tell the spy only what he needs to know—nothing more. And I feel the same way about writing for the screen. You tell the audience only what they need to know—no more. And as little of that as possible. I feel that a great deal of tension can be given to any scene, any character, by keeping the information to a minimum."
— Walter Brown Newman, *The Screenwriter Looks at the Screenwriter*

Stopping and Starting

If you want to vastly improve your screenwriting, here's a simple, inexpensive self-study program.

1. Study as many screenplays as possible.

Reading screenplays and studying the films produced from them is an excellent way to improve your work. What will serve you best are copies of the actual screenplays as they were written for production. These may be ordered from a number of specialty sources in Los Angeles and elsewhere. If you can't find the actual production scripts, order the published scripts of films you admire from your local bookstore or one of the many online bookstores. There are also several magazines that publish screenplays. My personal favorite is *Scenario*, which publishes two or three screenplays (as well as interviews with top screenwriters) in each issue, and their presentation is excellent.

2. Lay out a game plan—a selection of study scripts (movies).

To start your study-viewing program, select somewhat randomly a dozen movies that are available on video or DVD. It doesn't matter if you have seen them before. If you have, so much the better. However, you should not focus on a single genre, and you should include some of the classics from the American Film Institute's list of the Best 100 Movies (as with most courses of study, you should be familiar with your history).

3. The first viewing: Get an overview of one of your chosen films.

View one of your study films from start to finish. This first viewing should provide you with an overview of the movie and prepare you for the closer stop-start study that will follow. Your goal is to study the screenplay, not the camera angles, the production, or the performances. Focus your mind on the script. If you have the screenplay at hand, so much the better, but it is not crucial. You should check your watch as you start the film or, better yet, place an easily readable clock nearby. Consult your clock regularly to determine when major events happen in the movie and how long it takes for these events to happen. Start the movie. As it plays, you should be aware of all of the following:

a) How quickly does the action line begin?

   How soon do you discover the protagonist, the character who will drive the story?

b) How soon are you made aware of who or what is the protagonist's opposition?

   How soon are the protagonist's problems introduced?

   How soon does the dramatic tension begin? (It will probably occur at the same time the protagonist's problems are introduced.)

c) How quickly are you aware that you are hooked by the story?

What surprises does the story have?

When does the story get complicated?

What obstacles must the protagonist overcome?

Who or what creates conflict (dramatic tension)?

d) How does the writer bring this story to a climax?

How much time does it take to wrap up the story after its climax?

e) When are you aware that the movie has a theme—a message that the writer wants to deliver about the story?

4. The second viewing: Study the same film scene by scene, using the "stop-start" method.

Run the film again. On this viewing, stop the tape or DVD at the end of each scene, pausing to reflect on the scene you just viewed before going on to the next one. This is a most important process. Take your time. As you study each scene, note the following:

a) How was the scene's dramatic tension created?

b) How much dialogue was needed to give the scene's necessary information to the audience (you)?

c) How much of the dialogue gave inferential information, and how much gave explicit information? In other words, what is flat-out told to you (naked exposition), and what are you led to understand?

How was the exposition of information made interesting?

d) Make particular note of what is not said—what is subtext. (Subtext is skillfully demonstrated in the award-winning HBO series *The Sopranos*.) What is not said is often the key to creating the audience's all-important need-to-know, which is what fixes the audience's attention on the movie.

e) Does the scene delay telling you things you want to know? What drives the scene forward?

What surprises does the scene contain? (Surprises are a screenwriter's greatest weapons.)

Was the scene itself a surprise?

What if anything was predictable in the scene? (One of the worst things that can happen is allowing your audience to get ahead of you.)

What is each character's attitude in the scene?

How is dramatic tension maintained in the scene?

How swiftly did the screenwriter move the story forward? (And how was this accomplished?)

How many lines of dialogue are in the scene?

What did the scene tell us about what's coming next? (Hopefully, nothing.)

5. Once you've completed the film's stop-start viewing . . .

After you have worked your way through a movie scene by scene, think back on the movie as a whole. Ask yourself how efficiently the story was told. Were you ever bored? If so, figure out when, where, and why your boredom set in. I can assure you that boredom occurs when dramatic tension disappears. Check it out. A movie cannot succeed without dramatic tension—which should begin on page one, if possible, and continue through the climax.

6. Repeat steps 3 through 5 for each of the twelve movies that you selected for your initial study.

Add one film per month. The more movies you study, the more you will learn about screenwriting. If you are dedicated, you can and will teach yourself to become a screenwriter.

When you have completed your self-study course in stop-start viewing, you will know how to look at a film the way professional screenwriters do. After a while, you will be able to analyze any film on a first viewing, without stopping and starting, and every movie you see will become a learning experience. The more films you study using this method, the more you will learn about screenwriting. I urge you to continue your self-study program until analytical viewing becomes second nature for you.

This self-education program will reveal whether you have a burning desire to become a screenwriter. If you don't, now is the time to bail out. People who devote themselves to screenwriting (or any of the other arts involved in moviemaking) usually do so because they are hooked on it, dedicated to it.

If you don't have that fire in your belly, if you just think it sounds glamorous to be a screenwriter, hobnobbing with the stars, living an exciting Hollywood lifestyle, forget it. It's not going to happen. Aside from the fact that screenwriters are rarely invited to glamorous parties or any of the hoopla associated with Hollywood, there is nothing exciting about writing a screenplay. It's hard work, and it's lonely work. And, once in a while, it's satisfying.

Body Heat

(a movie written and directed by Lawrence Kasdan)

I suggest you begin your "stop-start" (scene-by-scene) studies with the film *Body Heat*, a most aptly titled film-noir mystery that contains wonderful screenwriting lessons in every scene. I believe you will learn more from studying the videotape (or DVD) of this critical and box-office success than you will learn from any lecture on screenwriting. This is what teaching yourself to become a screenwriter is all about. And to do this, you've got to get behind the picture and see the words that were on the script's pages.

Following is my scene-by-scene analysis of *Body Heat*. You may read it as you pause between scenes or, if you prefer, you may read it before beginning. In either case, I have spelled out the principal lessons to be learned.

The single most important scene in every screenplay (movie) is the first scene. It must tell the audience what the movie is about, signal its genre, and establish the special nature of its protagonist. *Body Heat* accomplishes this perfectly. Screenwriter-director Lawrence Kasdan puts viewers in exactly the right place, forewarning them that they will be involved with an insatiable sex addict and that the subject of this movie is the emotional and physical heat of sex.

Kasdan opens with tall, handsome Ned Racine (William Hurt) standing in his boxer shorts at an open window, his half-naked body wet with sweat, watching a building burning on the horizon. The woman behind him, seen in her bra and panties, is putting her flight attendant's uniform back on. Ned has obviously just had intercourse with her. "It's hot. I'm leaving," she says. "You're probably done with me anyway." (Good dialogue gives information without resorting to naked exposition.) Ned, amused by her remark, moves toward the bed, laughing, "Where did you hear that?" Clearly, Ned wants more.

Sex is his addiction. We know this from the first lines of the first scene—an opening scene that takes less than one minute of film time, a half-page of script.

Kasdan has grabbed our attention immediately. The mixture of fire, hot weather, and sex is literally combustible. There is something dangerous about the scene. Violence is in the air. (The potential for violence often creates more dramatic tension than violence itself.) Note that Kasdan tells us only what we need to know to pique our interest, nothing more. This is a vital point. If you are to create and sustain the dramatic tension that holds an audience's attention, you must guard your surprises and maintain mystery throughout your screenplay.

The next scene, seemingly just an extraneous beat (Kasdan deliberately makes us feel that it is not important), establishes Ned as a not-very-good attorney. This is critical information, but Kasdan doesn't tell us why. Note that this information is revealed in a half-page scene of exposition through conflict. Conflict is the essential ingredient of all drama. No matter how short the scene or how little the information you want to show or tell the audience, you must do it with conflict. Conflict creates tension, the key to all drama. No conflict, no drama. (Also, no conflict, no comedy.)

In the brief scene in the lunchroom, opening on a shot of a wall-mounted air-conditioning unit, we are shown, not told, that this is probably mid-'50s Florida in the summertime. (In every scene in this film, heat is the ongoing, unbearable menace that plagues the characters.) We need no words. This is a good example of what you can do by showing (describing in your screenplay) what the audience needs to know without dialogue. Whenever possible, try to approach your scenes as if they were silent: What can I show instead of tell?

The setup ends after about two and a half pages of screenplay (two and a half minutes into the movie), and we are now into the storyline. It's a hot night. Ned, a man alone and on the prowl, aimlessly strolls the pier. In the background, we see and hear a big band (again, without saying it, we know we are somewhere back in recent time, even though the clothes, settings, visuals could be the present). The band is playing a popular song of the era, "That Old Feeling." The lyrics are not heard, but for those who recall them, they are, "I saw you last night and got that old feeling. . . ." Not a vital piece of information, of course, but note that screenwriters should indicate in their screenplays exactly the song they want in a scene.

Ned wanders about the pier, eyeing the scene, probably for a woman. We don't need to know—we are held by this character, this amiable loser with no place to go and sex on his mind. Then a beautiful woman in a billowing white dress leaves her seat, walks toward him and passes him by, seemingly oblivious to him. (The secret: He's *her* target. But Kasdan knows it is critical to his story that he not reveal this vital information.) Ned follows her; she is a sex addict's dream come true. Again, nothing is said. As so much of this screenplay, the silences are golden.

Ned decides to pursue her. Teasingly, she tries to fend him off, telling him she's a married woman. He is unfazed. His urge to have her grows stronger. She knows that she's got him hooked. We sense that this is a dangerous game.

When I interviewed my lifelong friend the late Walter Brown Newman (undoubtedly on the short list of the greatest screenwriters of all time) for *The Screenwriter Looks at the Screenwriter*, I asked him, "What general rules or guidelines do you follow for 'finding' a beginning, a middle, and an end?" His reply is the best prescription for three-act structure that I've ever heard. Walter said, "It has to do with decisions on the part of your leading character. The beginning has to do with the first big decision he makes that starts the story going.

And the middle has to do with some of the decisions he faces because of the initial decision he made. The end is the result of all those decisions." Walter's method is a blueprint for *Body Heat*. Study the movie with it in mind.

Ned's first big decision is to pursue this gorgeous woman (Matty Walker, played wonderfully by Kathleen Turner). He's hooked, no matter how many obstacles she puts in his path, and she puts up plenty. She lets him know he has to work for it. She has a smart-ass answer for his every gambit. But Ned isn't put off. Instead he relentlessly pushes harder, enjoying the challenge. CONFLICT = DRAMATIC TENSION.

Matty is simultaneously a come-on and a put-off. Her ambiguity fascinates us. We know she is up to no good. What is she after? We don't have a clue. The genius of this screenplay is that it appears to be an open story, perhaps merely a sexy lust story. But Kasdan makes certain that he guards his secrets. He tells us as little as possible. GUARD YOUR SECRETS. *Body Heat* will show you how it's done to perfection.

Kasdan knows that sex is the equal of violence for dramatic tension. The difference between them is that violence plays on our external, physical fears while sex plays on our internal, emotional fears. Both can be dangerous. And they are the two most important tools of your trade, but only if you use them wisely, judiciously. This screenplay exploits sexual tension better than any other script I have ever read.

While searching for Matty after she vanishes just when he thought he was making progress, Ned has a sexual liaison with a nurse. This is an M.O.S. (silent) scene. No dialogue is needed as we see a nurse in the background putting her clothes together in front of a mirror next to a rumpled bed. Ned is indifferent; he has had his fix for the night. Kasdan underscores Ned's sexual obsession without words. It's just an ordinary nightly fuck for Ned. But the nurse isn't Matty. And there is no need to say it. The silence tells you volumes about Ned Racine.

Next, Ned finds Matty. And after a brief bout of double-entendre-laden verbal sparring, she gives him permission to follow her home. There he makes a gentle, tentative move on her. She rejects him, telling him to leave her house. He stalls on her front porch, looks back, and sees her through the glass panels that frame her front door, moving provocatively, a woman clearly eager for sex. Ned needs only a moment before he grabs a chair and smashes the glass, rushing inside to take her. Such is the power of his passion that he immediately begins stripping off her clothes. They fall to the carpet, urgently groping as she pleads, "Please, Ned!" He mounts her at once, and their passion consumes them.

The exact moment when Ned shatters the glass and charges in like a bull in heat could be called the first-act curtain. It is Ned's fatal decision—the one that will destroy him. Ned's initial decision to pursue Matty is, as Walter Newman would put it, the protagonist's first big decision that propels the story. His second, bigger decision (resulting from his first decision to pursue her) is to smash in the door and ravish her. Kasdan has classically escalated the dramatic tension to this point of crisis.

I have sometimes noted in my screenwriting seminars that three-act screenplay structure is like sexual intercourse. Act one, page one, establishes the subject matter, in this case, sex. Within a few pages, the writer begins the metaphorical foreplay, which immediately starts the "rising action" (the escalation of dramatic tension), building excitement up to that first big decision: Yes, we're going for it. Act two is penetration, intercourse, action and reaction, increasing dramatic tension (and surprises, which increase the rising action), building to the orgasm, the literal climax at the end of act two. Act three is always the catharsis—the release of tension, the resolution. It is the briefest of the three acts.

When working in three-act structure, keep the sex analogy in mind and you'll not likely have a structure problem. And keep in mind Walter Newman's "decisions," which imply actions. The term "decisions" is specific, and brings with it much more dramatic impact than the term "turning points," a neutral academic term that tells you nothing. Always think "decisions."

We are well into the picture before we meet Oscar, the police detective, in the little lunchroom where Ned and his pal Assistant D.A. Lowenstein (Ted Danson) are having lunch. Lowenstein is not your typical assistant district attorney. In a nice bit of comic relief, he dances like Fred Astaire, without music, just because he enjoys it. And Oscar is no ordinary detective; he's an African-American philosopher who, along with Lowenstein, likes to needle Ned about his sex life. (Try to give all of your characters their own "beat," a distinctive trait that will make them interesting.) As Ned joins them, Oscar begins complaining about the heat and announces that in this kind of weather "people kill people," they "forget the rules." It is a neat piece of foreshadowing by Kasdan.

After yet another round of vigorous intercourse, Ned and Matty are lying naked and sweating in a bathtub, pouring ice cubes into the water, when Matty says, "He's coming back tomorrow . . . he's small, mean, and weak . . . I can't stand the thought of him." Ned's face registers the import of her comment. And we understand who she's talking about—her husband. We begin to suspect, as Ned does, that she has something sinister in mind. Nothing else needs to be said. Silence can power dramatic tension.

Ned is shown at his home, miserably alone in bed, looking at his all-too-silent phone. He needs her. No words are needed.

Ned drives out to Matty's house at night, sees the back of a woman who looks like her standing in the gazebo, and says, "Hey, lady, wanna fuck?" She turns around smiling, but she isn't Matty. Kasdan has decided he must crank up the second-act complications. So he adds a new and mysterious character, a pretty young woman. Matty says this lookalike is actually her best friend. But we are not reassured by her explanation. We sense that something phony is going on, but we don't know what. We have another little mystery within the mystery.

Kasdan cuts to Matty, nude, putting on a robe; Ned sits naked on the bed. They've obviously just finished yet another sexual marathon. Ned asks her, "How do you know?" She replies, "I've seen the will." This is a great use of shorthand. No exposition is necessary. The scene slides into talk of the murder of her husband. "That's what I want,"

Matty says, "what I've always wanted." "That's where we're headed, isn't it?" responds Ned. The word "murder" is never spoken, but we know where they're headed. It's much stronger, much more dangerous when unspoken, implied.

Matty tells Ned not to talk about it, not to think about it. It is a beautifully crafted scene in Kasdan's minimalist style. We begin to realize that Matty, by denying the idea of killing her husband, is actually leading Ned to doing it. Kasdan has cranked the tension up another notch. Ned will kill Matty's husband, at her instigation. Ned, already established as a not-so-bright lawyer, clearly doesn't know he's being set up. Gradually we become aware that this seemingly open story is, in fact, a closed story. Matty's hidden agenda seems too simple; we sense that something else is going on. But Kasdan keeps us guessing.

Throughout this exceptional screenplay, information is kept to a minimum. We are given solitary pieces of the puzzle that keep us involved, speculating, needing to know more. I've never seen this technique used more effectively.

The decision to kill Matty's husband is the beginning of act two—the "what goes wrong" act, where complications create unexpected situations while escalating tension. Matty's husband arrives home, but when he opens his car door, out steps a little girl of about six or seven! No mention of her in the screenplay until now; she's one of Kasdan's carefully guarded surprises. What's she doing here? What does she have to do with the story? "Don't worry, Roz will pick her up," the husband tells Matty, "and she won't stay overnight," referring only to the unmet Roz, purposely unidentified. Do we need to know who the kid is? Do we need to know who Roz is? Definitely not now—that would destroy the tension, the mystery. But Ned and Matty are upset by this unexpected turn of events because they know who the kid and Roz are, but they don't tell us, although it's clear that their plans to murder Matty's husband are now somehow made more difficult, complicated. These are all perfect second-act events.

One night soon after, dripping wet in his swimsuit, Ned suddenly appears on Matty's front porch. She rushes into his arms. Their passion for each other is overwhelming. Matty immediately sinks to her knees to give him oral sex when, out of nowhere, the child in her nightgown suddenly appears, staring at them puzzled and fearful. "Aunt Matty?" she asks. Frightened by what she sees, she runs back upstairs. Ned and Matty realize they have been caught in the act by her niece. Possible big-time trouble? Complications?

Cut to the child being picked up by her mother. There is no mention of the consequences of the child having seen them, nor of what this possible disaster will do to Ned and Matty. But, clearly, Matty is worried. The important lesson here, once again, is what is not said.

Ned shows concern as he enters a restaurant and asks for a table. Matty appears. Ned greets her with a familiar smile. Suddenly her husband appears behind her. Another one of Kasdan's many guarded surprises. Her husband, Edmund Walker (Richard Crenna), invites Ned to join them for dinner. Does the husband know Ned is fucking his wife? This embarrassing moment is played with perfect ambiguity: Maybe he suspects the infidelity, maybe he doesn't. Their dinner conversation is loaded with inferential dialogue. Edmund is vague about what he does for a living, but Matty interjects that he owns The Breakers. When she leaves for the restroom, Edmund and Ned are alone. In the midst of their light conversation, which plays tensely against our knowledge that Ned is planning Edmund's murder, Edmund, referring to his wife, says with casual menace, "If I thought she was seeing another guy, I'd kill him with my bare hands." Obviously both men have hidden agendas. We know Ned's agenda but not Edmund's. And Edmund, who is smooth, is clearly not a man to be messed with. We are held by what we don't know and aren't told.

The next day, as Ned enters his office, he's surprised to see Matty waiting for him. She says she's afraid as she moves into his arms and tells him how much she loves him. "We're going to kill him," Ned says, "and we both know it." (This is the first time that the idea of murder is openly stated.) Escalating dramatic tension. Kasdan is cranking it up.

We see Ned planning the murder, checking out the future scene of the crime, The Breakers, a ruin of a former beach hotel owned by Matty's husband. The dramatic tension comes from the danger of the enterprise: A cop car patrols the street out front. Ned is nervous but nonetheless self-assured. We remember that he's been established as a not-too-swift guy. Will the cops spot him?

Once again Ned and Matty have a postcoital conversation, and Matty mentions that they could get more of her husband's estate if they changed his will to eliminate his sister and niece. Complication! "Let's not get greedy," says Ned. He tells her it would be dangerous to change the will now.

Note how Kasdan uses a very interesting and effective technique throughout this screenplay: He backs into scenes. Matty is so cool she's almost reluctant to mention things like murdering her husband or changing his will. When you back into a scene, you hold back the key point of the scene, building to it, getting to it almost as an afterthought.

As the movie progresses, Ned is squeezed ever tighter, but he's powerless over his sexual addiction to Matty. Like all addictions, this one is damn near unbeatable. Ned is hooked bad. Raising the stakes with mounting complications is also creating the desired rising action, increasing the audience's involvement in the story.

The murder is told from the victim's point of view, which gives us the freshest and most interesting involvement in it. (For switching points of view mid-screenplay you must study the premier example, Joseph L. Mankiewicz's *All About Eve*.)

True to form, Ned damn near bungles the murder, yet somehow manages to kill Edmund. But it is also made clear that this is not the end of Ned's problem, just the beginning. Dramatic tension has escalated. The essence of almost every good act two: *Nothing ever goes as planned.*

Ned's troubles take a new and surprising turn. He gets a call from a Miami lawyer who tells him that Matty has submitted a new will, which was supposedly executed by Ned! This is news to Ned. He is frustrated, powerless. He can't reach Matty. He must attend a meeting in the Miami lawyer's office. There he meets Edmund's sister and discovers that both Matty and his friend Assistant D.A. Lowenstein, whose office is involved with the investigation of Matty's husband's death, have been invited to sit in. This scene is a tightly written example of how much exposition can be accomplished in just a few words. The squeeze on Ned—the tension in this scene—is palpable. Matty has done Ned in, and now he knows it. But there's nothing he can do about it; it's too late. This scene, like so many others in *Body Heat*, is masterfully written. Study it. You'll learn how to create and build tension with the minimum amount of words.

Following the meeting, Ned returns home to discover both Lowenstein and Oscar, the police detective, in his apartment, waiting to question him about Matty. Ned, squeezed still tighter, decides on a seemingly honest approach. He confides that Matty came on to him after the Miami meeting and that he's going to see her tonight and every night and weekend she'll have him. Lowenstein tells him, "Ned, someday that dick of yours is going to get you into a very big hassle." As often happens in movies, the theme is baldly stated to the audience. In this story, the theme and the action line are identical: Sexual addiction leads to self-destruction. The murder is only a peripheral part of the main action line (Ned is as hooked on Matty as an addict on heroin). A character with an addiction (to drugs, alcohol, women, gambling, you name it) is always a good story to pursue be-cause you have a built-in antagonist within the protagonist.

Self-destruction is one of the great themes and/or action lines a screenwriter can use to guarantee rising action, building dramatic tension to a climax. *Patton* and *Citizen Kane* are classic examples of movies with characters who in triumph still manage to destroy themselves.

Now Kasdan begins the dramatic process of peeling away layers of the backstory, feeding out information a few pieces at a time, as Matty's astonishingly devious plot unfolds. We see this from the point of view of the victim, Ned, as he realizes how cleverly he's been set up to take the fall for the murder. This is all third-act material, part of the resolution. And it is quite unusual because most third acts are very short resolutions. Kasdan, however, is in no hurry. He's got you, and he knows it. He can afford to take his time because he was so meticulous in setting up his audience, bit by bit, step by step. The depth and cleverness of Matty's deception is not revealed until the very last frame of the film. Only then does this screenwriter give up all his secrets.

You need no guidance from me to follow the last twenty minutes of this movie. I will, however, point out that each scene, like a piece of a jigsaw puzzle, adds another missing element to the portrait of an extraordinarily devious and clever woman, a black widow spider killing the male she mates. At the end of the film is a delightfully improbable twist, which you may protest is unbelievable. But so what? All movies are dreams made to seem real. Were you snared by it? Did it hold your interest?

Body Heat is a fresh approach, perhaps an homage, to *Double Indemnity*, a 1944 classic. With *Body Heat*, Kasdan shows us how to approach an old subject with a completely fresh point of view, with new plot twists and new characters and the freedom that screenwriters did not have in 1944. Only the barest skeleton of *Double Indemnity* remains. *Body Heat* is an original piece of work. Watch it and learn from it.

Learn Screenwriting in One Hundred and Nineteen Minutes

I t takes nothing away from the brilliance of Orson Welles' performance, direction, and production of *Citizen Kane* to note that there exists overwhelming evidence that he did not co-write the screenplay, as he is credited in the film. Herman J. Mankiewicz wrote the script alone, dictating it to a secretary as he hobbled around in a room at a guest ranch in Victorville, California (a two-hour drive from Los Angeles). Mankiewicz, a well-established screenwriter, was a notorious drunk who had been stashed away in Victorville to keep him sober long enough to deliver the script. But the writer had no taste for sobriety or dude ranches, which may have been part of the reason that he improvised the screenplay almost faster than his stenographer could take it down. Mank worked without a net. He had no outline. "I made it up as I went along," he later boasted. There is no evidence to dispute his claim.

Known in Hollywood as a very funny man, Mank was a star attraction at the weekend celebrity parties thrown at San Simeon, newspaper tycoon William Randolph Hearst's castle on the Central California coast. At dinners in the baronial hall, Hearst seated the screenwriter next to him so he wouldn't miss Mank's famous witticisms. But while Hearst was feasting on Mank's wit, little did he know that Mank was feasting on Hearst's lifestyle as material for a future screenplay. Hearst, practically the inventor of yellow journalism and an authentic scoundrel, gave Mank a great theme: Lord Acton's axiom, *Power tends to corrupt; absolute power corrupts absolutely.* It also neatly fit the character of Orson Welles. As Sara, Mank's widow, once remarked to me, "Kane was actually based on Orson Welles." Knowing Welles' tempestuous, flamboyant nature, Mankiewicz tailored Kane to his star's measure, as dramatists have been doing since long before Shakespeare tailored his parts to fit Burbage.

So the first lesson of this movie is that writers steal not only from life but from people they know. Mixing fact and fiction is their stock in trade. As the great drama scholar Eric Bentley remarked, "Drama is life with all the dull stuff taken out."

Mankiewicz could have chosen to play Charles Foster Kane's story in any of the five basic genres. His choice was comedy-drama heavily laced with satire, a larger-than-life style perfectly suited to his star, Welles. Although he had a great protagonist (Hearst) whose real life was legendary, Mank had to find a way to dramatize the story. He knew that scenes from the life of William Randolph Hearst, no matter how dramatic or colorful they were, would be a snooze. He had to find a strong line on which to hang all the dramatic scenes of this powerful man's life—something that would make it cohesive, make the scenes connect, something that would hold an audience's attention. Thus came "Rosebud," and a line of action was born. Once Mank had that, changing the names of the real-life characters and locales enough to avoid a lawsuit was a no-brainer. He was ready to tell his story, skillfully mixing fact and fiction.

Mank's first decision was to tell the story backward, beginning with Kane's death—a grand, Gothic-style death that instantly estab-lishes his protagonist's grandiosity. He opens on big, forbidding iron gates; a castle is seen on a hilltop against the last light of day, the camera slowly moving in on a well-weathered sign: "NO TRES-PASSING." Whether this was Welles' or Mank's visual pun is not known. But pun it is, since the story is based upon the life of a man who was a master trespasser and is about two reporters whose assignment is to trespass into the life of the departed Kane. The camera, having made its point, moves in through the gates of the dark old mansion, and a single light in an upstairs window blinks out. First images: faded grandeur, wealth, decay, isolation. Shock cut to an extremely tight close-up of an old man's lips as he whispers "Rosebud," and a glass snow globe spills out of the unnamed dying man's hand, clattering down the stairs and smashing. A nurse enters and covers the dead man's face. The story is instantly under way with a big, dramatic event and only one word of dialogue. The entire story is then based on the press learning the meaning of this man's dying utterance. How quickly can you start your action line? Instantly. One word and we're off and running.

Shock cut to *News on the March*, wherein Mank does the really outrageous: He shows us twenty minutes of naked exposition! Every screenwriter knows you just can't do that; naked exposition is the kiss of death, right? Wrong. Mank makes it funny (funny can always break any rule). In a parody of *Time* magazine's weekly theatrical newsreel series of that era, the highly popular *March of Time*, known for its pomposity and "Timespeak," he gives us Charles Foster Kane's obit, effectively and authoritatively showing us how important the dead man was, ergo how important this story is going to be. Mank knows that when you're going to knock down a high hat in the movies, it's best if that high hat is just about the biggest high hat there ever was. *Drama/comedy is the art of exaggeration, a most important lesson for every screenwriter new or old.*

The obit ends; Mankiewicz cuts to a dark, smoke-filled projection room where this rough cut of *News on the March* is noisily discussed by the guys who produced it. "What's Rosebud all about?" they ask one another. "What does it mean, if anything?" Some say it means nothing; others argue that it may hold the key to Kane's life. The newsreel, they conclude, is not just about finding the meaning of Rosebud, it's also about discovering Kane's secrets, the hidden story of the great man's life. These guys are tabloid journalists trying to dig up the dirt. They hope "Rosebud" is something hidden in old man Kane's past, something juicy that the public doesn't know. Note that Mank unloads all this naked exposition through *conflict*. Each character has an opposing view of what, if anything, Rosebud means. But their boss tells them go to hell and back to come up with something to titillate the public. Thus the reporters become detectives, and the movie becomes a mystery story.

But the screenwriter's tricks have just begun. This story will be told in flashbacks within flashbacks, all seemingly random. But, of course, they are not. "Rosebud" holds this free-for-all together. I've seen this movie many, many times, including its first theatrical release in New Orleans in 1942, yet I never know which scene is coming next. And my bet is that neither did Mankiewicz as he dictated it. Although he had notes, there is no doubt that the script was improvised. And "Rosebud" is the glue that holds it together.

Citizen Kane still dazzles us today in large measure because of Welles' extraordinary performance and direction as well as the unusual German Expressionist style of cinematographer Gregg Toland. But the key to the screenplay was to dramatically set up Kane so that the audience would want to know the inside story, like seeing a supermarket tabloid unfolding before their very eyes. Thus Mankiewicz took an extraordinary amount of time setting up Charles Foster Kane as a Very Important Person, a commanding figure. We're both awed and fascinated by ruthless and powerful people, and we cheer when they rise and cheer even more when they fall. Flamboyant antiheroes are just plain fun to watch. Larger-than-life characters, if properly exploited, will carry a movie, a comedy or a drama, all by themselves (think *Patton, Gandhi, Tootsie, The Godfather, Erin Brockovich*, et al.).

Of all the movies that you put on your "stop-start" screenwriting program, put *Citizen Kane* first. Here are a few specific things to look for as you watch it:

Note Mankiewicz' economy in getting in and out of scenes. He has a consistent ability to enter an already underway scene at its exact dramatic (read emotional) peak. Every scene in this screenplay starts on an action. *Something is happening right now.* A good example is when the trustee of Kane's inheritance comes to take young Kane away. This scene begins with the trustee saying "I think we'll have to tell him now." Mankiewicz makes the audience want to know, "Who is this guy? What is this scene about? Why does this man want to take the boy away?" This is a classic example of the "need to know" principle. Begin a scene at a high point, starting with something already in progress, skipping the introductory stuff when possible. Make the audience *need* to know what's happening, withholding information as long as possible.

Kane's mother says, "I'll sign those papers now, Mr. Thatcher." Audiences are immediately caught up and held by the scene. Viewers ask themselves, "What papers? What's going on here? Who are these people?" "You seem to forget that I'm the boy's father," the other unidentified man in the scene says to Thatcher, thus introducing himself to the audience. Yet we still don't know what the hell is going on, which is just the way the screenwriter wants it. Need-to-know holds an audience and whets its curiosity. In this scene the need to know also involves an unidentified child seen playing in the snow outside the window.

"It's going to be done exactly the way I've told you, Mr. Thatcher," says the woman who we're beginning to realize is the boy's mother. Still, Mankiewicz doesn't tell us what they're talking about because he wants to keep us guessing, keep us involved. The father says, "He owed the money for the board to both of us. Beside, I don't hold with signing my boy away to any bank as '*guardeen*' just because . . ." What's he talking about? We don't know. Something very important is going on, *but the writer will not tell us. He's guarding his secret.* Mankiewicz is feeding the audience just enough (a child is being taken away from his mother and father, but we don't know why). He teases us with inference, which is a useful way to gradually reveal a hidden agenda and increase the audience's need to know. Unlike the naked exposition of the newsreel, Mankiewicz has turned sly, reverting to one of the most successful tricks of the screenwriters' trade—teasing us with bits and pieces of information, holding our attention, being deliberately oblique. In moments like these, screenwriters can find nuggets of pure gold. Look for them as you watch movies. It's the hidden agenda that often hooks an audience.

Writers can learn so much from this little-noted but critical scene. Exposition in this scene could have been deadly, so Mank avoided it altogether. He already had spent so much time setting up Kane in the newsreel that he now had to move the story along. So he artfully danced around the dull legal proceedings by conveying only their *dramatic results*. He knows the dramatic meat of the scene, so he can leave out the fat. We witness only the drama of a child (the young Kane) being taken away from his parents by a man named Thatcher. The child is taken away because he inherited the "Colorado Lode," whatever that is, and that's all Mankiewicz ever tells us. The name Charles Foster Kane is not mentioned because it's not needed. *Remember, tell your audience only what it needs to know, and as little of that as possible.*

By the way, the unnamed but featured sled that Kane clings to as he's about to be taken away from his parents is, of course, "Rosebud." In this scene, however, we don't see the name on it. Mankiewicz won't tell us that, of course, because it's the solution to the riddle of "Rosebud"—his foremost secret—which will not be revealed until the last frames of the movie.

Now we leap ahead in time and find the same Thatcher who took Kane from his family reading a newspaper in Kane's office. Kane, indifferent to this bore, his former guardian, leans back in his chair, smiling insolently, his feet on his desk. Twenty years have gone by, but no calendar pages flutter on the screen, no sign reading "Twenty Years Later" appears, none of the conventions are used. Mank, way ahead of his time, is now in an even greater hurry. To hell with tired old conventions; he wants to keep his story moving. And we realize that we have to pay attention if we want to keep up with it. This pioneering technique is used by most screenwriters working today. And whatever happened to the reporters searching for the meaning of Rosebud? Who knows? Who cares? Mankiewicz didn't give a rat's ass about structure. His mission was *storytelling*.

This first scene with the grown-up Kane establishes his verve, arrogance, self-confidence, and flamboyance. Kane is a young man who gleefully thumbs his nose at the establishment. He's a very charming rascal. He's capable of doing anything. He's been expelled from several colleges and is amused by this "accomplishment." Mank wants us to note immediately that the key aspect of Kane's character is his willfulness and his irreverence. Nobody and nothing is going to stand in this young man's way. He will shape the world to suit his immense ego. The scene is about two and a half pages in length. But it tells us what kind of character Kane is. Watch out, Mank is saying, this guy is explosive; he's going to be difficult, fun, and *unpredictable*.

Those of you who think that the three rules of screenwriting are (1) structure, (2) structure, and (3) structure, please take note. There is only one abiding rule: *You cannot be boring*. Great screenwriters grab the audience by the throat and won't let go. The best structure is whatever you decide it is for whatever story you happen to be telling at the moment. Your structure should vary to fit each story. One size does not fit all. In writing *Citizen Kane*, Mankiewicz obviously didn't subscribe to any structural formulas. Fortunately, there were no screenwriting teachers to tell him how it should be done. Ignoring all the unwritten "rules," Mank focused on letting his story (i.e., his character) take over, keeping the pace fast and furious, using flashbacks within flashbacks, spewing out scenes like shotgun pellets. This was daring stuff back in 1940, and still is today. (Read Scott Frank's screenplays and see his films. He is obviously the previously unacknowledged heir of Herman J. Mankiewicz.)

Abruptly shifting gears to a slower pace, Mank's shorthand storytelling style is epitomized by his montage covering the nine years of Kane's first marriage. Kane and his wife are seated at the breakfast table, where they exchange only a few words. He's preoccupied with his newspaper. She wants some attention. Dissolve to the same scene, different wardrobe—sometime later. They're still seated in the same chairs at same table. Kane's preoccupation is turning to annoyance (we know he's begun an affair with Susan Alexander). Dissolve to an unspecified time years later, and they're no longer speaking to each other. The set and costumes have been only slightly modernized, and the couple remain seated in the same chairs at opposite ends of the table. In each of these successive scenes, the couple is found sitting farther apart, the growing silences between them telling the story. It's the most famous set piece (quite literally a one-set piece) montage in movie history. With little dialogue and big silences, we are shown the degeneration of a nine-year marriage. It's tour-de-force screenwriting at its finest. Decades before Harold Pinter and David Mamet (little doubt they both studied him), Mank understood how "less is more" works for screenwriters.

At some point during the writing of *Citizen Kane*, Herman Mankiewicz must have said to himself, "What the hell, go for it." I can't imagine a better way to approach a screenplay. The lesson here is to trust your guts, your instincts. Forget paradigms and steps and whatever bullshit is thrown your way by well-meaning but non-screenwriting teachers and lecturers. It's your life; it's your screenwriting career.

Caution: Do not approach this peerless classic with solemnity or awe. *Citizen Kane* is not a museum piece. It's fun, it's theatrical, it's dazzling moviemaking. It's a riproaring, popcorn-eating movie that Pauline Kael called "an almost Gothic comedy." And she's right on target.

"There are things that one learns about structure . . . I mean, the conventional wisdom is the war between plot and character. . . . I don't think that that war is quite that way for movies. I think that it's more of a three-way war . . . what somebody would do and, I guess, what you'd like them to do in order to keep the goddamn thing going. But also, there's something else. . . . I don't know quite how to put it, but it's a little bit like music. And that's the greater war, really. I mean, in writing a screen-play . . . you just sense a movement. . . . It's like jazz musicians improvising, or if a movement is . . . allegro, then the next one should be lentamente . . . or something like that. . . . You can call that structure. . . . I don't know what you call it, and I guess this sounds vague . . . but, ah, I don't think there are principles, other than asking yourself over and over again, 'What's going to happen next?' . . . and seeing if you're interested in what's going to happen next."
—Robert Towne, from *Word Into Image*
(courtesy of American Film Foundation)

Big Talent from the Redneck Riviera

An Interview with

Robin Swicord

"As a writer, you must have a commitment to having two jobs: the job that keeps you alive and the job that you love— writing—which you have to do unfailingly and obsessively to get good enough so that you can actually succeed."

—Robin Swicord

This is a unique story of strength, courage, talent, and risk-taking in equal measure. I can't imagine a better recipe for becoming a top-of-the-line screenwriter.

The daughter of a naval officer and a mother who was an aspiring writer, Robin Swicord grew up in a series of small Southern towns, devoting herself to reading and developing her talent as a writer. "I just wrote constantly," she tells us. After studying theater and literature at Florida State University, she set off alone on a daunting odyssey into the wilds of the New York City, hoping to meet filmmakers. The important lesson here is that those who have the courage and determination to go for their goals in life, ignoring the odds against them, are the ones who have a shot at winning; those who are cowed by their fears of failure haven't a chance. Case in point: Robin Swicord, who went her own way, became a first-class screenwriter, and is in the process of becoming a superstar screenwriter and, very likely, a director as well.

Upon meeting this young woman, I was impressed by her aura of serenity, quiet strength, and self-assurance. It takes no crystal ball to see an extraordinary career ahead for Robin Swicord.

FROUG: Did your screen adaptation of *Little Women* propel you into the major leagues?

SWICORD: Yes. I had one screen credit before it, but *Little Women* was the first movie to be made that represented just my work.

FROUG: How did you happen to get that assignment?

SWICORD: It was an assignment that no one wanted or believed in, as is so often the case with movies that become successes. When Amy Pascal and I met, she had just gotten her first job in the film business, working for a producer, and I had sold a number of screenplays, but I had not had any of my movies made yet. When we met, we talked about doing an adaptation of *Little Women*, and then we walked around trying to get people interested in it, but no one was.

FROUG: Did they all say that it had been done before?

SWICORD: It had been done before, and who cares? A couple of studios said, "We don't do costume dramas." Amy and I felt that the book is important for a lot of girls and young women. Even though it is antiquated, it still is a wonderful depiction of adolescent life and girls moving toward autonomy, and it has quite a bit about ambition. It begins with these girls saying what their dreams are, and by the end of it, everyone has had some kind of dream come true. It's a classic for a reason. Amy and I both felt that a true adaptation had never been made; what it's really about had never been made. But we couldn't interest people here, because here there was and still is a bias against making movies with a female protagonist.

Over the years, Amy and I just never forgot about making a film of the book. Twelve years after our first discussion, Amy was working at Columbia Pictures, and the last several pictures that she had been responsible for had been the only hits Columbia had in the previous year. She had a little bit of clout. Not enough to green-light a picture, but enough to call me up to say, "I think the time is right." And I said to her, "I don't want to do this unless we are really going to make the movie. You have to promise me that, no matter what, we will make this movie." She swore to me her blood oath, and she and I got together and started talking about what this film should be. We went through the book page by page and talked about women today and about what from this book still needs to be said today. I spent about six months doing research on it and then wrote a first draft. Amy was a just a tireless champion of this at Columbia Pictures, and other people there slowly came on board. It was only made because the right movie star said yes and because we figured out a way to make the movie on a fairly low budget for a studio. In fact, while we were shooting, they continued to take money away from us.

FROUG: It was a big hit, wasn't it?

SWICORD: I would say it was a moderate hit. It was Columbia's big movie of the Christmas season, and they were very happy. I was happy. We all were. It continues to have a life because a lot of people have bought it on video.

FROUG: It's one of the few remakes that they said was better than the original.

SWICORD: Well, it's wonderful that some people felt that way. I never thought of it as a remake. I think that when a book is a classic, you can return to it at any time and make an adaptation of it for the current time.

FROUG: When did you begin writing?

SWICORD: I have been writing quite seriously since I was six years old. I wrote a novel when I was fourteen. I just wrote constantly. I tried to take jobs that did not take all my energy, so I could come home at night and write. As a writer, you must have a commitment to having two jobs: the job that keeps you alive and the job that you love—writing—which you have to do unfailingly and obsessively to get good enough so that you can actually succeed.

FROUG: As a young woman growing up in a small town in Florida, what led you to screenwriting?

SWICORD: As I was growing up, I never imagined that I would make films. I didn't even know that people made movies. I wasn't exposed to a lot of movies, except what was shown on our local unaffiliated station. It didn't belong to any particular network, so it would just buy its programming, including a lot of old Hollywood movies, which it cut up to insert lots of commercials. So, oddly enough, I was exposed to some of the greatest films that had ever been made in the '30 and '40s.

FROUG: Even though they were cut up like sausages?

SWICORD: For me it didn't matter because I was seeing great performances and great writing and great direction. It's not the best possible way to see movies, but I saw all of Hitchcock before I was fifteen years old. I loved movies. And I sometimes had the experience of watching something on television and thinking

"I have been writing quite seriously since I was six years old. I wrote a novel when I was fourteen."

they should have done that differently or this scene would have been so much better if so and so. My mind was already working towards the understanding of film. At the same time, I was writing—always writing. Because of my love of reading, I imagined that I would end up writing novels. But when I got into college, I was exposed to more film—this time not cut up with commercials. I was also exposed to a lot of photography, because I worked for a newspaper, in their photo department, which is how I put myself through school. So I began to understand that what I had in my head were images and that what I had a feel for was the drama in human behavior. Although I loved language, I loved images more. My training as a journalist and as sort of a beginning poet was toward concision—to make images and to distill them. I took those sort of strands of ability, without really knowing if they added up to anything, and I started trying to write for the screen.

FROUG: How old were you when you started writing screenplays?

SWICORD: I wrote my first screenplay when I was about twenty-five. I was out of college. I was working in a quasi-journalist, quasi-educational-film world in a small-town kind of way. First I went up to Atlanta, where I made a small training film for IBM's General Systems Division, and they introduced me to their advertising people in New York. So I was offered a job at a tiny ad agency in New York, and I went to work there, writing for IBM. But my impulse for going up there was to meet filmmakers and become a filmmaker.

FROUG: How did you go about meeting filmmakers in New York?

SWICORD: I truly have an angel. I was so naïve. I would meet a cameraman on a commercial shoot and say, "I want to make a movie." And we would talk. No one encouraged me. You never should get that idea. People said, "Oh, you can be a script girl on the set." There weren't any female directors in America yet. There was Lina Wertmuller, but that was about it. It was kind of an unheard-of thing in the late seventies. If I had been realistic in any sense, if I'd seen the big picture, I might never have tried. But I didn't really know any better: I had lived a kind of weirdly sheltered, bookish, small-town southern life. I just figured this was possible. So I went around and talked to different people, and I finally figured out that the only thing that separates the person who's making a film from the person who's not making a film is money. The people who were making films had financing. But when I realized that, I really had no access to any kind of money. And I didn't know anyone who had any money. And I didn't know why anybody would give me money. So instead of making a movie, I wrote a stage play, which some friends and I put on in a little Off Off Broadway theater with ninety-nine seats. My first play was called *The Last Days at the Dixie Girl Cafe*. And that play made a tiny splash in New York and got published. Then an agent contacted me and said, "Have you ever thought about writing for the screen?" So I sent her the first thirty pages of a screenplay I was working on, and she said, "You should finish your screenplay." So I finished it and gave it to her. In a few weeks she had sold it. That was Merrily Kane, and she is still my agent.

FROUG: When was that?

SWICORD: 1980.

"No one encouraged me. You never should get that idea. People said, 'Oh, you can be a script girl on the set.' There weren't any female directors in America yet."

FROUG: Because *Little Women* was such an artistic achievement, did it help you break through the gender discrimination?

SWICORD: I think that quite a lot of gender discrimination still goes on, so I can't say that I broke anything. I think that before *Little Women* came out, really no one was vocally making the argument that women went to the movies. Of course, we know that Hollywood generally was and still is quite a bit a boys' club. People would say that *Beaches* was a fluke or *Terms of Endearment* was a fluke. Anytime there was a movie that had a predominantly female audience going to see it, it was considered a fluke.

On *Little Women* I was able to go into the marketing department of Columbia and argue that it's not a fluke that women make up half the audience for *Lethal Weapon*. There is a reason, and it's not because they want to see guns going off. I said it's because Mel is so cute. We have always supported films, but we are tired of seeing movies in which we do not see ourselves on the screen. It is so rare to go to a movie and see an honest and real portrayal of what a woman is and does. As it turned out, the person who was in charge of marketing there, Sid Ganis, had four daughters, and he agreed with me.

FROUG: Do you think that the gender gap has improved?

SWICORD: It has improved. I can't really say that *Little Women* was a watershed movie because there had been movies before it that were aimed largely at women and had gained even greater audiences. But at the time of our release, we were able to talk in the press about the fact that women did go to movies. And after that there arose a whole genre of these kinds of movies that we began to hear referred to rather derogatorily as "chick flicks." It was the first time that the term kind of entered Hollywood's consciousness. It's unfortunate that they say those kinds of things, but they say the same kinds of things about movies that are aimed predominantly at African-American audiences as well. Anybody that the mainstream has marginalized, they think of as niche audiences, as somehow less fans. I think that the success of not just *Little Women* but other movies for female audiences has opened the door a little bit more for more women to make the movies that they are interested in.

FROUG: Are you active in Women in Film?

SWICORD: I haven't been. I have nothing against them, but I am very involved with my kids' school. I sit on the school's board of trustees, and between writing and raising my family, I haven't given myself over to this kind of political action group.

FROUG: What draws you to a story? What makes you say, "I want to write this"?

SWICORD: Usually I respond emotionally to work. Usually there is a preexisting interest in something, even if I am not aware of it. When I come across the material, something awakens and I begin to think about it, even against my will. Then characters and voices begin to emerge, and I know that I am going to write it.

FROUG: What drives you first—the story idea or the characters?

SWICORD: I think it's different for each project. In *Little Women*, Jo was important to me, as she has been to so many women writers, and I wanted to honor that book and Louisa May Alcott by giving her a new adaptation. In other things, I see a situation that my heart just responds to or something that strikes me as so funny that I think I would have such a good time writing it.

FROUG: Let's take *Shag*, a funny and charming film. Did you say to yourself, "This will be great fun"?

SWICORD: Right. *Shag* was an interesting opportunity for me. I normally don't rewrite people; I turn down rewriting work all the time. But this was a script that came to me through a friend. And I knew I could do it because I had grown up in a little town, Panama City Beach, in northwest Florida, which is called the "Redneck Riviera," and I knew a little bit about Myrtle Beach because my mother is from South Carolina and my cousin was shag champion of Columbia, South Carolina. I knew that there were enough similarities between Myrtle Beach and Panama City Beach in the summer that I could write it. And I had an impulse to write about my childhood, especially what it was to be about ten or eleven years old, looking at the teenagers of the early sixties dancing together. I wanted to write about teenage rituals and to capture that part of my childhood, but the script, which was quite funny in its own way, was not a film that was going to get produced in its current form. It was pretty clear to me and to the others who had read it that someone would have to rewrite it.

I tried to change as little about the characters as I could, but I changed everything about the story, because it was not working. I was able to sort of take characters from the draft that I had read—a lot of which was about a group of boys who want to buy alcohol and find girls, which we've seen in movies like *Porky's*, in which the women are objects and fragments of people who never could exist—and do the flip side. I wanted to elevate that kind of teen comedy and to show it from the other side— the girls seeking their freedom and bonding in friendship, which I had never, ever seen on the screen. So I used their script as a place to begin and did a complete and total rewrite. I do absolutely acknowledge the original writers' contributions. I never would have come to this project and written about a shag contest if they had not found it for me, but I put so much of my humor and my world in it. And I knew those girls so well. They are still so real to me that I find myself wondering what they are doing today.

FROUG: What struck me most about *Shag* is how little human nature has changed. I have three daughters, and any of my girls could have been in there. What was the toughest screenplay you've written and why?

SWICORD: Well, I think the toughest screenplay I ever worked on is *The Curious Case of Benjamin Button*. It has largely been tough not because of the writing but because of the particular journey that this screenplay has been through—with so many people trying to develop it into something it is not. And it has not been produced yet. I am working on it with yet another director, and I am, once again, hoping that it will be made. But I don't know what will become of it.

FROUG: How much time will you give to this?

SWICORD: I don't know. It's been a ten-year process. I don't know how many drafts I've done, maybe fourteen. Every time I have to return to that script, which has been taken away from me twice,

I think it has got to be the last time. But it's like a child that still needs me, so I continue to work on it.

FROUG: How can you have a perspective at this point?

SWICORD: Because I am very strong-willed and I really hold on to what I know about the story and, particularly, about the character of Benjamin Button and about this century and about the opportunity to tell a story which spans the entire century.

FROUG: Who is Benjamin Button?

SWICORD: *The Curious Case of Benjamin Button* is a short story that was written by F. Scott Fitzgerald when he was about twenty-six years old. It's a very small short story that begins in the Civil War days and ends in the jazz age. It's about a man who was born an old man, instead of an infant, and ages backwards until he is an infant and, in his "old age," dies as a baby. The idea of man aging backwards is actually older than that story. Merlin had the same quality. But I wanted to use that idea as Fitzgerald had used it—writing it so that the man would end up dying in his era. So I wrote it so that the man would die in my era, which spanned the entire twentieth century, and I decided that he would be a musician because I could collapse time through music.

I wanted to write about what it is to be misunderstood—to have people look at you from the outside and not know who you are, which I believe is the human condition. I wanted to write about this man who feels himself to be a freak, to be different, and yet his story is completely universal. All the things that happen to him in his life unfold just as they would to anyone else, except he carries this great secret.

"I wanted to write about what it is to be misunderstood— to have people look at you from the outside and not know who you are, which I believe is the human condition."

FROUG: You're a wonderful writer, and now you are branching
off into directing. Why?

SWICORD: I really never have viewed writing and directing as
being separate for me. When I first went to New York, it was to
be a filmmaker. I declared from the very beginning that I
wanted to make films and direct them. But being able to direct
was not an option for me when I first started, so writing was
something that I did because I could do it. At the point that I
began to be taken seriously, my first children came along and I
didn't want to be away from them, so I deferred that time
when I would begin to direct. My children are older now, and I
can begin to focus on directing.

It is impossible for me to write without imagining the full-
fledged film. I see the film, as so many writers do. It's disappointing and quite disheartening that it is so hard to find a
collaborator—a director who will work with you as a contractor
works with an architect, trying to make something beautiful
together that is an adequate reflection of the intention of the
writer. So often, I feel the auteur theory, which Nick [Kazan]
calls the "hauteur" theory, has been harmful to films. I fault it
tremendously because very good work is distorted and made
into very bad work through that idea. Almost all writers would
love to have a director who would work with them, develop a
common vision, and make a movie together with them. Then
writers who are not temperamentally intended to direct would
feel a kind of satisfaction as artists because the work they intended actually was getting made.

I think that I've always been headed towards directing. A few
years ago, when I finally directed a short film about my grand-

"I really never have viewed writing and directing as being separate for me."

mother, the actual making of that film was, for me, a compilation of all the things I have ever loved in terms of making a room beautiful, understanding something about fashion and the language of clothes, the spatial sense that I have, my interaction with other creative people, not just the actors, but the other artists I work with—the director of cinematography and the musicians. I have a strong response to music, and to be able to cut a film knowing that I was going to work with the person who was going to be scoring the film was wonderful. When I was in the very final stage of doing that and picking out little sound effects, I loved listening to each little effect, to the qualities of this one as opposed to that one. I felt so fulfilled. Someone said to me, "Only a director would love to sit in a room listening to different doors closing, hearing which doors convey exactly the emotion needed for the moment." I think there is something true about that for me. I love that detail.

FROUG: How are you progressing in the directing area?

SWICORD: It has been an interesting year for me because I had an offer to direct a movie that I wrote, but when I got all finished writing it, the studio felt that the movie was too small and too different from the kind of movies that they wanted to make.

FROUG: They couldn't spend fifty-two million dollars on it?

SWICORD: They couldn't spend fifty-two million dollars on it, and it made them nervous. I don't fault them. I mean, I knew from the very beginning that this was going to be a movie that was too small for them, but their enthusiasm for it was such that I felt, "We'll go down this road for a while and see what happens." This year I have been working with an independent producer.

We have found financing for the film as of now, and we have made offers to movie stars. If movie stars say yes and we are able to put this together, we will make a movie and find a distributor and try to get this little film out there. If movie stars are not attracted to it, the movie won't be made.

FROUG: When movie stars are involved, your low budget will go to hell, won't it?

SWICORD: I don't know, we'll see. It's not a very high-budget film. I don't have to have the biggest stars in the world for my size budget.

FROUG: Do you plan to continue to write when you are not directing?

SWICORD: Yes. I don't have to direct every single thing that I write.

FROUG: What is your favorite film that you have done?

SWICORD: The film that is closest to my intention is *Little Women*, and I would say *Shag* is a close second. There are things that should have been shot for *Shag* that the director did not understand. When I see the film, I still feel their absence.

FROUG: If you had it to do all over again, would you?

SWICORD: I don't really feel that I have a choice. This is what I came here to do.

FROUG: *Matilda* was a really wild and woolly experience. Did you have fun doing it?

SWICORD: It was a mixed experience. But the writing was a blast. Planning the movie and writing it was so much fun. The making of it, the production part of it, was most difficult.

FROUG: Why was that? Did the director have a different vision?

SWICORD: Yes, I would say so. But in the end, quite a lot of the movie is as we intended. There was a gulf between our sensibility and Danny DeVito's sensibility, and over that gulf there were quite a few battles fought. We lost some of them. Some of them we didn't, because when Nick [Kazan] and I sold the screenplay, because it was a spec script based on a Roald Dahl story, we had gone to the Dahl estate and made arrangements with them. The screenplay's underlying rights were tied to the book's underlying rights. In selling it, we got something put into the contract that is never put into screenplay contracts, which was that we could not be rewritten. The studio could not have us rewritten—no matter how much the director wanted something different—without losing the rights to the book.

FROUG: Like a Dramatists Guild contract?

SWICORD: It was like a Dramatists Guild contract. But we did not try to hold on to every single word or moment. We really did try to be good collaborators. But when some things seemed to us to be very far off the mark from what we intended, we could say no.

FROUG: Do you think that the movie was too broad?

SWICORD: It was, for our taste, a little too broad and a little too violent. At the same time, when you look at Danny DeVito's other work, it is of a piece—there is a certain sensibility that all of his work has—and you can't go into business with the foreknowledge that someone's sensibility is so strong, so marked, and later complain, "Gee, it wasn't what we intended." We did know, but Danny was very strongly Mrs. Dahl's first choice for director, and we definitely respected him and said, "We're going to make this collaboration work." It's just always difficult in a business where there are a lot of strong egos. It's often difficult to get everybody lined up together and working towards the same thing. I think that there are places in the film where we are very together, and then there are places where things are more extreme than Nick and I, if we were directing it ourselves, would have made it.

FROUG: When writing your screenplays, do you work in three-act structure?

SWICORD: I think about the story unfolding in three beats: a beginning, a middle, and an end. But I don't conform to any particular formula where things have to fall on a certain page and so forth.

FROUG: You don't believe in a paradigm?

SWICORD: No, I don't. Film is so organic, and each story has its own way of unfolding. But there are certain things that we know to be true. We know that movies are roughly two to three hours long, that comedies are shorter than dramas, and that the middle is longer than either the beginning or the end. You sort of roughly aim for that.

FROUG: Most members of the Writers Guild are appalled by the possessory credit—"a film by . . ."—by which directors dump on writers. What can be done about that?

SWICORD: The shortest route would be for writers simply to withhold their services because, obviously, they can't shoot blank

"Film is so organic, and each story has its own way of unfolding."

pages. However, it is very hard to get the entire Guild mobilized around some of these issues. The Writers Guild's function is to provide a minimum basic agreement. The minimum basic agreement does not cover most of the work that is being done in Hollywood today. Mostly, only a hundred or so writers find their work represented on the screen right now. The minimum basic agreement is not particularly good for the people who are outside of that group.

The only way that we could make our power felt so that we could reason with people and say that the possessory credit is a lie—the film belongs to no single person, certainly not just the director when the writer has imagined the screenplay and worked for years to bring their vision to the screen—is for the entire guild to step aside and let the people who do most of the writing that appears in feature films be allowed to strike without the fear that other writers would simply come back behind them and do their work. I think that we can never achieve what needs to be achieved for writers until writers stop rewriting each other. When writers honor each other's work and refuse to do the studios' bidding and refuse to rewrite and change another artist's work, then we will have real power.

FROUG: I agree with you one hundred percent. Look at what happened at Columbia. A few major screenwriters went over there and negotiated their own deal for a piece of the gross.

SWICORD: That's right. There are other things that are now in the works that are similar to that. But it's difficult because writers who want to be working a lot and want to have screen credits—and I have certainly spent years in that position—get angry about this kind of talk because it's viewed as elitism. The longer view is that it will be good for all writers.

FROUG: It's not elitism because a percentage of the gross, now already enjoyed by 250 screenwriters, is open to any new or established screenwriter who qualifies.

SWICORD: That's right. It is a group that any writer can join. Anytime that your work is so accepted or is honored in one way or another, you are automatically in that group. People who are worried about possessory credit are people whose work gets made, and they feel insulted when they see "a film by Gillian Armstrong." In fact, it is not a film by Gillian Armstrong. Many talented, creative people made that film. People who are not writing screenplays are not as much offended because it doesn't affect them. They have other employment concerns.

FROUG: The history of the Guild has been that the only thing that gets a strike vote is money.

SWICORD: The creative rights issues are more important to writers than to anyone else. Directors have a lot of creative rights as it is. So they have other things to be concerned about besides creative rights; they have their own problems working under a corporate studio system. But within the Writers Guild, only a minority of writers is concerned about creative rights. The others are more concerned about employment access, and I agree with that. But, as Guild members, we sort of find ourselves at odds with each other, unfortunately, and there is a lot of distrust among writers.

"The creative rights issues are more important to writers than to anyone else."

FROUG: It's basically the old fight between the haves and have-nots.

SWICORD: That is exactly what it is, and I have sympathy on both sides, having been on both sides. But the truth of it is if we want movies to be better, if we want our original visions to be more intact, then writers will have to cooperate and respect each other more.

FROUG: What do you think young aspiring screenwriters should do today?

SWICORD: The advice I would give young writers is that they should, above all, write. It's hard to write well. It takes a long time. You have to write badly for a number of years before you can even begin to start to have control of your craft. The most important thing is to really spend the time sitting in a chair at the computer writing, and to not be critical of your work until after you've finished it. Once you've finished it, you must be critical of your work and move between two modes: generating work and being creative and sitting back and assessing it and showing it to a lot of other people, so that you are not writing to any one person's notes but are getting a general portrait of where you are in your ability. And at the point when you simply can't stand it anymore, you have to get out of where you are and try to pursue your work in New York or, preferably, Los Angeles, where screenwriters are employed.

"You have to write badly for a number of years before you can even begin to start to have control of your craft."

FILMOGRAPHY

1980   *Kill Castro* (shared credit)
1987   *You Ruined My Life*, television movie
1987   *Shag* (shared credit)
1988   *Little Women*
1989   *The Perez Family*
1990   *Matilda* (shared cedit, with Nicholas Kazan)
1998   *Practical Magic* (shared credit)

A Couple of Screenwriters with Fresh POVs

An Interview with

Robin Swicord

and

Nicholas Kazan

"You shouldn't be doing it in order to speculate, hoping to get rich. You're not a prospector in the hills of California in 1849. You are somebody who wants to tell a story. In my experience, when a writer tries to figure what the market wants, tries to think of the ideas that are most likely to sell, and writes those ideas, the results are not very good and no one buys it. But if the story you are compelled to write really excites you, inflames your imagination, and continues to hold on to you—tenaciously— that's the story that you can best write."

— Nicholas Kazan

Undeniably, homes very often reflect the character of their occupants. A good example is the residence of screenwriters Robin Swicord and Nicholas Kazan. Peace and harmony are the words that leapt into my mind as I was welcomed inside and the three of us sat down at a big wooden dining table in a large room that overlooks Santa Monica Bay in the distance. Although I was a stranger, I felt totally at ease, soaking in the ambient goodwill and good cheer.

FROUG: How is the current market for screenwriters?

SWICORD: I think the availability of work for established screen-writers is good. For the screenwriters who have not gotten themselves well established yet, I think it is harder.

FROUG: Why?

SWICORD: When I came into writing for the film business, selling my first screenplay about 1980, there was a tremendous amount of development that went on. So at that time, even though I wasn't a very good writer, I would be able to find work. I was in a sort of earn-while-you-learn mode. That doesn't really happen anymore. The studios are less willing to give beginning writers a shot.

FROUG: They no longer develop ten scripts and end up producing one?

SWICORD: I am sure the ratio was higher then. I knew a development executive in 1981 who told me that he was personally supervising 200 scripts that year.

FROUG: Of which maybe one made it to the screen?

SWICORD: Maybe one.

KAZAN: They have done all kinds of cost/benefit analyses of development, and every analysis shows that they were wasting their time. So now studios are concentrating on the very established screenwriters—I mean, just the cream of the cream—and everyone who is below the very established screenwriters is having trouble. There is a group of screenwriters that meets informally on Thursday nights. At the last meeting, we had very well-known writers who said that they were having trouble finding work. These are people who have worked steadily and are used to turning down job after job. So I think it's really difficult to find work now.

FROUG: Is this because the average budget is now fifty-two million dollars per picture?

KAZAN: It's partially because the average budget is very high, but it is also partially just what the studios' research found. If they have a good idea and they give it to a very good screenwriter, they're likely to get a script that they can shoot. If they give it to someone else, they are afraid that they're going to get something they can't shoot. I think they are making a mistake. There are a lot of really good writers who should be working who are having a difficult time finding work. But executives have always been primarily concerned about their own jobs. No one will fire them if they hire an A-plus-list screenwriter, but if they hire someone else and pay them "only" five hundred thousand dollars and the person does a bad job, then the executive looks bad.

FROUG: Do we have still a booming rewrite industry? Are you all rewriting each other's screenplays?

KAZAN: I think that industry is booming, but Robin doesn't participate in it at all and I do very minimally.

SWICORD: There is, unfortunately, more and more of a trend right now to go to sequential writers. The studio will pay a lot of money for a first draft of a screenplay, and go to a very established writer to get that draft. Then, when they have the movie star and the director, they do a rewrite—a rewrite for the movie star and a rewrite for the director. And maybe another for another movie star. Then the executive starts to get worried. Maybe it's not funny enough, maybe it's not scary enough, so they start bringing in writers who are quite expensive, whose job is largely to cannibalize other writers' work. They just come in and tinker with somebody's original work.

FROUG: They're paid like twenty-five thousand a week?

SWICORD: Much, much more than that.

KAZAN: People are now getting from one hundred to two hundred and fifty thousand dollars a week.

FROUG: To do a rewrite?

KAZAN: This is only for production polishes. The film is going to be made. You don't get that if they just say, "We have a bad script. We need you to rewrite it." But if they are in preproduction and they know they are going to be making the movie, then they feel, in essence, that any money that they spend which leads to an improvement is worth spending. Of course, as Robin points out, very frequently they don't get an improvement at all.

FROUG: Eric Roth says that you can't really significantly improve a script when you come in and do just a couple of days' work.

SWICORD: No. What it does is erode the power of the artist's voice. The first writer who comes to it has a lot of authority, because he or she creates something that never existed before it sprang fully formed from that writer's imagination. So anyone coming behind is basically doing the studio's bidding. Sometimes the studio can't make the first writer execute the studio's notes if the ideas are poor. The first writer may not be willing to accommodate the studio and take the risk of that material actually ending up on the screen. So people will come in for a few days, really as guns for hire, to do almost anything. They have nothing invested in the project. They get a lot of money; they walk away. I call them the people with big houses, because they make so much money from doing that. So many of them privately moan and say, "Gee, I need time to get to my real work." It's as if they have made a bargain with the devil, because if what you are doing is simply coming behind other writers and walking over their scripts to accommodate the studios, then you are not spending your time doing your own work as an artist.

FROUG: But they're making easy bucks?

"The first writer may not be willing to accommodate the studio and take the risk of that material actually ending up on the screen. So people will come in for a few days, really as guns for hire, to do almost anything. They have nothing invested in the project."

SWICORD: If that's really all it is, own up to it. Face it, don't weep and moan about what you're doing.

KAZAN: I just want to stay on this for one second. The truth is, there are many kinds of writers and many kinds of scripts. If you have an artist writing a script, as Robin suggests, the best solution is to stick with that artist until that artist finishes and to keep nudging that artist, keep making suggestions. Some of those suggestions may not bear fruit immediately, but may bear fruit in a year's time. The writer may do two more drafts and suddenly they are able to entertain an idea that they couldn't entertain before, because they see it from a new perspective and are able to realize it.

But there are other people working in Hollywood who are just trying to make a buck or just trying to sell an idea. They are smart enough to have a good idea, but they are not really writers. In those cases, I believe that you need to have a writer come behind and realize the idea.

The problem is that the studios can't make the distinction between these two kinds of screenplays and see where they have to stick with a writer even though there may be "problems." Often these problems are insoluble. Often these problems are obvious to anyone who looks at the screenplay. And often they don't make a damn bit of difference when the movie is made, because the movie has an original voice, so the audience won't care about the problems. The problems may be there, but the audience says, "I love this movie anyway. Yes, I guess that was a 'problem,' but the movie had such originality and spirit that I don't care that there was a 'problem.' "

SWICORD: I have had films of mine made that were so far from what I intended that I was sick with disappointment. But I have friends who say, "Oh, I really loved it. I saw you so much all through that film." Something has survived that people who know me are able to detect. So I guess that there are some things, some residue, that survives.

KAZAN: Strong ideas, as you suggest, leave a strong residue, but you also have to acknowledge the tremendous fragility of art. The thing that distinguishes a good film from a really good film and a good film from a poor film is the accretion of a lot of small moments that work properly, in which case the film can be good or very good or great. Or, if enough of those little things miss, it throws off the story and you are not involved anymore. You turn against the story. You become angry at it.

FROUG: But the writer is really powerless once the director and the star say, "We want a dog in here. I'd like to have horses in the script. I want scenes outside where I can show my ranch and charge it against the picture budget."

KAZAN: Well, yes you are. But if you are still involved and it's your original story, you can say, "I can figure out a way to work a dog in here." You can say, "I can figure a way to put this scene outside." There are ways to transpose your original vision and put it in another location, as Robin did in *Little Women*, to adjust for budget problems. You may have to condense three scenes into one, but you figure out a way to do it. However, when these decisions are being made in a haphazard fashion by a subsequent writer or by the director and the actors working together and improvising, you end up with something that doesn't work.

"The thing that distinguishes a good film from a really good film and a good film from a poor film is the accretion of a lot of small moments that work properly. . . ."

[187]

FROUG: It wouldn't surprise me if a certain executive who left Disney wouldn't have said, "I want to see the little women getting it on. I want to see them take off these Victorian costumes. I want to see some sex."

SWICORD: We are immune to bad ideas because we hear so many of them. On the other hand, writers also have a lot of bad ideas. This is the hard thing as a writer. When I was talking to our lawyer this morning, he said that he tried to play piano for a year and a half during his twenties, but he made so many mistakes he couldn't stand to hear himself play. I said, "When you work in a creative profession, you begin to understand that it's always about imperfection and that you never reach perfection." Even having perfection as an ideal is absurd.

In a collaborative mode, we expect to hear an idea and to come out with another idea ourselves and somehow be able to work together so that we will finally arrive at something that we are happy about together. Unfortunately, the way things are set up creatively right now—and I hope we will change it in the film business—the person who is doing the most important original creative work, the writer, is the person who can be fired for disagreeing with an idea or for having tried something unusual in a script. "Let's see how this would go," we might say to ourselves, and we take a risk and write an interesting original thing. When you can be fired simply for having thought outside of the box for a moment, it has a tremendous dampening effect on the work itself. And then people complain because movies are bad. They have a right to complain about it. But there is very little that writers themselves can do to change it unless we

"We are immune to bad ideas because we hear so many of them."

change the economic structure of the film business, which is essentially that it's corporately owned and the same kinds of people who make decisions about selling soda pop and theme rides make decisions about what kinds of movies get made and what their contents should be.

KAZAN: The dangerous thing is that the fundamental belief in our culture is in a sort of perfectibility of the individual. Certainly there is a belief in Hollywood in the perfectibility of the screenplay. I think that's a very dangerous idea. Because, as Robin suggests, nothing is perfect. No human being is perfect. No screenplay is perfect, and when you try to take out the imperfections, you are frequently taking out all the originality and all the life.

We don't hate studio executives. Studio executives are grossly overworked; they don't have time to spend two days reading a screenplay, thinking about it, trying out options. They have to respond off the cuff and often, as Robin suggests, they have some bad ideas. They are not to be faulted for those bad ideas. Everybody has bad ideas. We have a billion of them, but we try them out and discard them. As a writer, you try to make those bad studio ideas work. You feel that, because they're coming from the person who hired you, you have some mandate to make them work. But you always have to step back and remember that bad ideas are symptomatic. They're symptoms of a problem. So you have to say, 'I think you are telling me that the second act is too long. I know there is nothing wrong with the second act, so I have to take it out of the first act, because if I take it out of the first act, then we will get to the second act sooner and the

"The dangerous thing is that the fundamental belief in our culture is in a sort of perfectibility of the individual."

second act won't be too long." A million times you have to make these judgments, and you have to go back to the studio and say, "I have tried your ideas, and they don't work. Can I suggest something different?" Frequently they don't remember what their ideas were, because it is two weeks later, so they say, "Don't worry about that. Whatever works for you."

FROUG: So there is some room for you to fight back?

SWICORD: It really depends on the studio and what their impetus is. I had a project at a studio that was bought by another studio. The people who inherited the project had no real stake in the movie and their ideas were beside the point; they showed no understanding of what the intention of the film was. They only made the movie because movie stars had already committed to it. There was nothing I could say to this particular group that would convince them that their notes were not going to work. They ended up making a rather poor movie out of it, using other writers to do their work.

KAZAN: What's so amusing is that they are desperate for us because, without a good story, they will never get the twenty-million-dollar actor. Once they have the twenty-million-dollar actor, they don't want to see us, hear us, know our name. But when they are starting out or when they have a script that doesn't work or when they have just bought a book, it's "Oh, my goodness, who's going to write this?" They are desperate to have someone who they think is good, because without that, they will never get the other people they need. It is an interesting combination of disrespect and respect.

FROUG: They have contempt for you because they need you?

KAZAN/
SWICORD: [in unison] Exactly. Yes.

FROUG: Writers—especially the leadership of the Writers
          Guild—need to understand how vital they are. You can't shoot
          120 blank pages. If we really understood that, maybe we would
          use our power to gain recognition. But, unfortunately, writers
          seem to be basically shy and unassertive people.

SWICORD: We assert ourselves all the time. However, you have to
          remember that what we are up against is a very large umbrella
          corporation that owns bottling companies, theme parks, record
          companies. Now they are buying all kinds of Internet and
          electronic media companies. Their tentacles are everywhere. But
          they are not interested in making a contribution to culture. So
          TV and film, which right now make arguably the largest contri-
          bution to the culture, are in a sense being held captive by
          corporations who do not always care what messages they put out
          through the media. They just want to sell.

FROUG: Are we moving to the point where one corporation
          will own everything?

SWICORD: It's a horrifying state. The time when the most interest-
          ing movies of the last fifty years were made was after the studios
          had been broken up by the advent of television and before the
          corporations bought the studios. Those movies of the late sixties
          and early seventies were independently financed, usually under tax
          shelters. They were released by the studios, but you didn't have a
          lot of overhead that had to be supported, and the movies could be

"The time when the most interesting movies of the last fifty years were made was after the studios had been broken up by the advent of television and before the corporations bought the studios."

[191]

made without movie stars. People could take a chance on an idea. When you read the interviews with writers in Patrick McGilligan's books *Backstory 1*, *2*, and *3*, published by the University of California Press, you realize that the halcyon days of the last fifty years were the brief period when nobody owned anything and people could just get up in the morning and make a movie.

KAZAN: I think the period ended with the making of *Raging Bull*. I think it existed, in a sense, because the screenwriters didn't have studios giving them thirty pages of notes in the old days. The studios read a script and said, "We will make it" or "We won't make it," and maybe, "I think the girl should be younger." That was it. Those were the notes.

FROUG: But the studios were still fanatic about wanting to please the public. They were merely not interested in selling soft drinks and theme parks or distilling booze.

SWICORD: Or product placement or any of a thousand other things. It was not "We should make this movie because later we can make a ride based on this it." The old studios were audience pleasers, but they also knew that they were people who were making contributions to popular culture.

FROUG: Are there any encouraging words you might have? I don't want to create a totally bleak picture for the newcomers who read this book. What would you do if you were a young screenwriter today? Would you write a spec script and get it out there on the market?

SWICORD: I would definitely write a spec script if I were interested in being a filmmaker, because you are not going to get in through any other way. A spec script is number one. And number two is one of the things that keeps us enslaved in the corporate culture—we, as artists, have to do what we do. We can't stop. Other people can quit their jobs and go to work for a telecommunications firm or whatever. But if you are a person who is driven to write and what you see in your head are movies and nothing else, you have to do that work. It isn't as if there is another film business that we can go to instead. This is the film business, and, as a filmmaker, you're going to have to work here.

FROUG: You have to live in Hollywood?

SWICORD: That's right. But, at the same time, I think we have some responsibility once we are here to try and change the business in whatever small ways we can, by whatever kind of small activism we can mount against the monolith. And I think that the way movies will be distributed in the not-too-distant future could put power closer to the hands of the people who are making movies, because we will not need giant studios to distribute the films. There are already many smaller financing companies that are financing films either alone or in partnership with studios. So if the money is held in the hands of a lot of different people who want to make movies . . .

FROUG: You might get diversity?

SWICORD: Exactly. Distribution is something that is now tightly held by the five major corporations. I think that there will be a time dawning—unless Microsoft or someone snaps everything up—when we could create a culture that is so much more varied.

FROUG: Then we will hear individual voices?

SWICORD: Yes. That's something I am holding out for.

KAZAN: What Robin is referring to is that we seem to be moving toward a time when films will be shot digitally, so lighting needs will be minimal and the editing will be inexpensive. Anyone will be able to do it in their own home with very modest equipment, and films will be delivered to theaters not in tins and not on celluloid but electronically. If that is true, and it seems that that's what's going to happen, then the cost of making a film will be greatly reduced and the cost of distributing a film will be reduced. Anyone will be able to make a movie and get it delivered. You will advertise it on the Internet. People will then call your Internet site and you'll deliver your movie to their house or to a movie theater electronically.

FROUG: The film will be delivered to a theater electronically?

KAZAN: Yes. But to come back to your earlier question, Bill, I think that the only way to begin is to write spec scripts or just to write scripts. Writing a "spec script" implies in some way that you are hoping to make a million dollars off of it.

SWICORD: Speculative.

KAZAN: Yes. You shouldn't be doing it in order to speculate, hoping to get rich. You're not a prospector in the hills of California in 1849. You are somebody who wants to tell a story. In my experience, when a writer tries to figure what the market wants, tries to think of the ideas that are most likely to sell, and writes those ideas, the results are not very good and no one buys it. But if the story you are compelled to write really excites you, inflames your imagination, and continues to hold on to you—tenaciously—that's the story that you can best write. No matter how peculiar it is, the people who are reading one dumb cop/buddy movie after another will pick up your script about a little boy who falls in love with his grandmother and proposes to her or whatever—it could be the most peculiar thing—if the script is really touching. And that reader will hand it to someone else to read, and that person will say, "Yes, this is really good." So no matter how odd your passion is, your enthusiasm will carry the day and you then will have a chance to break into the film business.

JOINT FILMOGRAPHY
(For individual Swicord and Kazan filmographies, see the end of each writer's individual interview.)

1994   *Matilda*

"Although knowledge of structure is helpful, real creativity comes from leaps of faith in which you jump to something illogical. But those leaps form the memorable moments in movies and plays."
— Francis Ford Coppola

"You just have to write from your heart. Although your friends and your family will tell you it's not commercial, and the agents will tell you it's not commercial, you just have to go ahead and write it. If you write it from your head or from your wallet, forget it."
— Anna Hamilton Phelan, *The New Screenwriter Looks at the New Screenwriter*

"The writer is the most important person in Hollywood, and we must never let the sons of bitches know it!"
— Irving Thalberg

Rooting It Out

Lucky for us, there were no studio executives, agents, or screen-writing teachers around to warn William Shakespeare that he had to create "rooting interest" in his protagonist to hold his audience. The Bard would have been told to abandon his play *Richard III*, about a conniving hunchback who murders his nephews in order to be crowned king. Dick was one evil dude. Did you root for him? No way. But he was one fascinating sonofabitch!

Richard III was the basis for one of the first feature-length mov-ies ever made. And it has been remade again and again over the years. Sir Laurence Olivier filmed a version in 1955 that has become a classic. Check out the 1995 version, based on the National Theatre's production, in which Richard is transformed into a '30s Hitler clone. It's one hell of a good movie. More recently, Al Pacino took a stab at the man in *Searching for Richard*, a film that, if not spellbinding, is at least interesting.

Great movies often have protagonists who are as unsympathetic as they are fascinating. (To twist a famous F. Scott Fitzgerald quip: Show me an antihero and I'll show you a movie.) You can get a lot of mileage out of fascinating antiheroes. In *Get Shorty*, the protagonist, Chili Palmer, is a petty hood turned self-proclaimed movie producer. Screenwriter Scott Frank lets you know right away that Chili is one bad guy you don't want to mess with, which is precisely his fascination from the very beginning. Do we have a rooting interest in him? No, but he's fascinating.

More and more top-level contemporary screenwriters are realizing the fascination we all have with the dark side of human nature. Quentin Tarantino made an enormous splash with a little movie called *Reservoir Dogs*, in which terrible people do terrible things. He followed that with *Pulp Fiction*, another exploration into the dark side of human nature.

Paul Schrader is a screenwriter who made his mark early in his career by exploring humankind at its most dangerous level. In 1976 his *Taxi Driver* made a huge impression on the filmmaking world. Do we have a rooting interest in his sociopathic protagonist? No way. But we also can't take our eyes off him. Throughout the movie, he's a rattlesnake coiled to strike at any moment. This character builds tension because he's dangerous. We are held by his potential for violence. Schrader, who often explores the dark side, recently did it again with *Obsession*, which won Nick Nolte an Oscar.

Leaving Las Vegas, written by Mike Figgis, won Nicolas Cage an Oscar for playing a self-pitying, mean-spirited drunk. There's no rooting interest in the character, but what the writer created is much deeper—he exposed the character's inner pain for audiences to see and feel.

Consider a few must-see classics: Do we have a rooting interest for Charlie Kane, the power-mad, despotic tycoon in *Citizen Kane*? Certainly not. But we understand his frustrations, and he is surely one of the most fascinating characters ever created on film.

In *Unforgiven*, David Webb Peoples created the great screen character Will Penny. This outlaw got away with multiple murders, yet you are riveted to him. The plight of this widowed pig farmer with two young kids to raise and feed is Peoples' opening scene, establishing immediately that his protagonist is having great difficulty merely existing. Empathy is the screenplay's first note; whatever follows is built upon this foundation. There is no rooting interest for any of the male characters in this screenplay. Whatever rooting interest there is is saved for the whores. The movie won Best Picture and Best Director Oscars. I think it deserved a Best Original Screenplay Oscar as well.

Francis Ford Coppola, try as he might, did not quite manage to create a lovable Mafia family in his *Godfather* series. But his characters hold us not only because they are dangerous but also, ironically, because of the recognizable dysfunction of their family lives. Coppola, working from Mario Puzo's novel, understood that the key to his adaptation was to establish the humanity of the family members. By focusing on creating recognition and empathy, he presented the Mafia's business as merely an offshoot of the family itself. (Just an ordinary Italian immigrant family that happens to contain the head of a Mafia family.)

If you want to dramatize unsavory characters, your first priority is to dramatize their humanity: How are they similar to us and people we know? David Mamet's *Glengarry Glen Ross* is populated by foul-mouthed, unethical real estate agents desperate to outdo each other. Rooting interest for these deplorable characters? No way. But Mamet dug deep; he made you feel these characters' desperation to make a living, to survive in a brutal business world. The movie's theme is survival.

A noteworthy coincidence is that most of the characters in non-rooting-interest screenplays act out of desperation. Frank Pierson understood this when he wrote his two most famous screenplays, *Dog Day Afternoon* and *Cool Hand Luke*. To write *Dog Day*, Pierson had to dig deep into Sonny, his protagonist, to find his fatal flaw, which gave Pierson the opportunity to build empathy for the character. Once he had discovered Sonny's character defect, he could write his brilliant script.

American Beauty, an Oscar-winning dark comedy by Alan Ball, is an outstanding example of how to create characters who are singularly unlikable, miserably unhappy people. Yet they connect with audiences who understand as well as empathize with their misery. Ball, a TV sitcom writer before he dazzled Hollywood with this screenplay, clearly understands the primary truth of comedy: Laughter results from recognizable human pain. He bypasses superficial rooting interest, achieving the deeper connection of empathy. How does he do it? He dramatizes his characters' humanity—warts and all.

In Woody Allen's *Sweet and Lowdown*, his protagonist, Emmett Ray, "the second greatest guitar player in the world," is almost all warts. Egocentric and emotionally unavailable, he is the personification of what a great screenwriter can do when ignoring likability and rooting interest. This socially inept kleptomaniac is not only funny, he's also deeply vulnerable. The picture's humor plays off the irony that Ray has no awareness of his crude, insensitive behavior. He has only the conviction of his talent as a guitar player. Allen's screenplay proves that empathy, not likability, is what really creates audience interest and involvement, and that irony is one of the screenwriter's greatest tools.

The best screenwriters understand that they can get as much, if not more, dramatic tension and excitement from bad guys as they can from good guys. They also recognize that with growing audience sophistication comes the general recognition that none of us is pure good or pure evil. It's surprising that more beginners haven't grasped that if you want to stand out from the crowd and make your mark, you should try writing about the dark side, and throw rooting interest back into your writer's toolbox. Creating rooting interest for the good guys is a no-brainer; creating empathy for the bad guys is good writing.

What you want to get from your audiences and your screenplay readers is involvement with your characters. This involvement comes from three primary sources: recognition, fascination, and mystery (what might they do next?).

A tip on developing characters with greater dimension and fascination: When shopping around in your mind, choosing characters for your story, search for their defects. We all have them, some more than others. Character defects yield rich story material. If a character is not flawed, leave him or her alone.

Another bit of advice: Defy fiats. If anybody—agent, studio exec, teacher—lays down the rule that you've got to have rooting interest, ask him or her why. Rooting interest is the stuff of Hollywood-speak; empathy is the stuff of great drama.

The Next Big Step

Until you are an established, successful screenwriter, you will need to sell your work and yourself in order to get an agent and also to convince that agent to keep working for you after you've signed a contract with him or her. Getting an agent might not be as difficult as writing a screenplay, but it will definitely try your patience and test your stamina and creativity. Your first step down this path should be to check among your friends and acquaintances to see if any of them knows anyone who knows anyone who works at a Hollywood agency (or has a cousin of a cousin who works at an agency). Hollywood functions on contacts or, as they're called in the business, "relationships." In Hollywood, who you know is often more important than what you know.

Do not consider any agency that is not located in the film capital. Your agent must be on the scene in Hollywood, where film deals are made. If you live in New York, do not use a New York agent for your screenplays. Hollywood agents do not like to split their ten-percent commission and will not put your screenplay on their top priority list if another agency is also representing it.

Contact the Writers Guild of America, west, and purchase a copy of their list of signatory agents. The phone number for their Agency Department is 323-782-4502; the WGA's website is www.wga.org (to reach their agency page, click on "agents"). Study the WGA's signatory agency list carefully. It is an excellent resource, but it is not complete because some signatory agencies have requested that the WGA not publish their names. To make up for this shortfall, you might wish to invest in the Hollywood Creative Directory's *Agents & Managers Directory* (www.hcdonline.com; phone 310-315-4815).

Some agents list themselves as managers, promising that they will also manage your career. By so doing, they circumvent the California state regulation that limits agents to a ten-percent commission.

Managers often get fifteen percent of your writing income or higher. I do not recommend a manager for new screenwriters. Once you get a career going, you will be in a better position to decide whether you need a manager. Most screenwriters get along fine with just an agent.

There are three basic types of agencies for screenwriters: big, powerful agencies; small, screenwriters-only agencies; and small agencies that are not devoted exclusively to screenwriters.

Large, powerhouse agencies with numerous agents and diverse client lists, such as International Creative Management (ICM), Creative Artists Agency (CAA), and The William Morris Agency, are, to a great extent, "packaging" agencies. They use their major actor, writer, and director clients as elements to be combined and sold to a studio as a "package." These agencies will take a big commission off the top of the package; it far exceeds the ten-percent commission that they would ordinarily receive for a deal for any one of their clients individually. Their pitch to you is that, since they are collecting a packaging commission off the top, they will not charge you a commission for your screenplay because it's part of the package. Being part of a package is a mixed blessing: The studio may like the star and director but not your screenplay, in which case you're out.

As mentioned above, CAA and the Morris Agency, among others, have asked the Writers Guild not to publish their names in its agency list even though they are WGA signatories. This suggests that these agencies don't want to see new screenwriters' work, which is not true. They merely want to limit the material they see to that which has been recommended to them by other Hollywood professionals—in other words, pre-screened scripts. Yet in their thirst for a winner, they frequently look at material that arrives without an insider's recommendation. So you should not be discouraged from calling or sending an introductory letter to these agencies, requesting that they read your screenplay. (CAA is at 9830 Wilshire Blvd., Beverly Hills, CA 90212; phone 310-288-4545. The Morris Agency is at 151 El Camino Dr., Beverly Hills, CA 90212; phone 310-288-7451.)

Smaller agencies that exclusively represent writers generally hustle harder and are more likely to give you personal attention. Although these agencies often have to go to the major agencies to get screenplays into the hands of big-name stars and directors, some of these "boutique" writers' agencies have a great deal of power because they represent the top in-demand screenwriters.

There are also many small agencies that aren't screenwriter specialists but can do a wonderful job representing you. They have to work very hard to stay in business and are therefore a little more flexible about taking on new screenwriters.

The big agencies and the small agencies have their respective advantages and disadvantages. What matters most at this stage of your career is just landing an agent. You can always change agencies somewhere down the line.

Submit your screenplay to any agency whose response suggests an open-door policy, but make sure they are a legitimate operation. As you approach agencies, *always phone before sending material.* Besides establishing a contact person, your call should help you determine whether an agency is legitimate. Find out who they represent, how long they have been in business, etc. Don't target just one agency. You will increase your chances for success if you investigate as many as possible.

Your single most important weapon in your search for an agent is the telephone. When you call agencies, ask the person who answers to connect you to a new agent's office. New agents are always trying to make a mark in the industry, and a hot new screenwriter could be a big feather in their cap. When connected to an agent's secretary (or assistant), inquire about the agency's policy regarding new screenwriters. Try to start a friendly conversation without making a pest of yourself. Talk a little about yourself and your determination to become a screenwriter, but not about your screenplay. Your screenplay's subject must, for the moment, remain a secret. Your job, until an agent agrees to read your screenplay, is to sell yourself. If you are friendly and charming and not too aggressive, you will establish your first beachhead. Ingratiate yourself. With luck, you will actually be connected to an agent. Once connected to an agent, give him or her only a teaser about your screenplay—a preview, as it were, of coming attractions—just enough to tantalize the agent, to lure the agent into reading it. Always leave a little mystery.

Expect uneven results from your phone calls. Some who answer agency phones are cold, officious, and unfriendly. On another day, with another receptionist, you may be greeted warmly and courteously. It will likely take months to get an agent, but if you hang in there, eventually you will succeed. Every day of the week, new screenwriters are signed by one agency or another.

Some agencies state that they will only read a letter, not a screenplay. Do not ignore these agencies. Paradoxically, as forbidding as they like to appear, they desperately need new screenwriters. A great letter can seize a reader's imagination and entice an agent to want to see your screenplay. Your letter is your audition as a writer. Make it short (keep it to a page or a page and a half) and funny (especially if you are a comedy writer). The purpose of your letter is not to sell your screenplay but to sell yourself as a writer. You will be judged by your letter. It must be entertaining!

In your letter, do not under any circumstance synopsize your story. Give only enough of your story as is necessary to intrigue the reader, such as the story's genre, its title (only if you have a very good one), and your major cast ideas. Do not give alternate titles: Uncertainty suggests that you don't know what you're about.

Submit your letter to several agencies at the same time. By the quality of the responses you receive and some follow-up phone calls, you can determine which agency seems to suit you best. If you get no responses, make follow-up phone calls and/or reexamine your letter (perhaps you need to write a better one).

When you are ready to send out your screenplay:

- Do not put it in a fancy or specially bound cover. That will only mark you as an amateur. Use a conventional cover page and, of course, a conventional script format.

- Register your screenplay with the Writers Guild of America, west, before you mail it to anyone.

- Send your screenplay by priority mail. Your script will stand out from the routine mail.

- Keep a log of the agencies to which you've sent your screenplay (or letter) and the date on which you sent it. Wait two weeks after the date you calculate the agency received your script and then phone them, merely inquiring whether your screenplay was received. (This acts as a subtle reminder to them to read it.) Log the date and time of your call. Once an agency has had your screenplay for a month, phone again and ask for the person with whom you have had previous phone contact. Inquire whether your screenplay has been read and, pressing on a bit, ask who has read it and if you can speak to that person. Even if you don't get through, you've now put them on notice that your patience is wearing thin. This second call is usually the one that prompts one of the agents in the office to read your script.

To protect themselves against false claims, all agencies will insist that you fill out a release form before you submit material to them. Do so. It only guarantees that, in the event of a dispute regarding your screenplay, you agree to submit to judicial arbitration.

A fact of life in Hollywood is that everyone in the film industry is looking for a filmable screenplay. But paradoxically, everyone in the industry hates to read screenplays (except for those who are paid to do it). Experience has taught them that most of the screenplays they receive are poor or dreadful and are often rehashes of old movies or tired, formulaic stuff. So, if you write a fresh, exciting screenplay, the big, forbidding gates of Hollywood will fly open as if by magic. In my forty-year experience as a writer-producer in Hollywood, I can tell you that, to my best knowledge, no good screenwriter has ever failed to get an agent. *Don't give up.*

And the Winner Is...

How desperate are they?

Production companies that continue to announce that they will not read a screenplay unless it is submitted by an agent now read screenplays that somehow slip in under their doors or are brought in by gate guards or tour guides or friends of friends of distant cousins. While most producers and studios insist that the old submission rules still apply, their eagerness for good scripts has escalated to the point where they are much more relaxed about enforcing them.

Now, more than ever before, producers and studios actively scout for screenplays. So smart screenwriters invent and exploit their own opportunities. Anybody who is creative enough to write a screenplay should be creative enough to develop a strategy for either using the system (through an agent) or getting around the system (through alternative channels).

I believe that the single most important career step for an aspiring screenwriter is to come to Hollywood and begin networking as quickly as possible. Contacts—plus talent—are the keys to a successful screenwriting career. Stories of screenwriters who came up with ingenious ways to get their screenplays read by key people could fill a book. It's not a mystery; it's merely putting your creativity to work for your career. When I interviewed screenwriter Anna Hamilton Phelan for *The New Screenwriter Looks at the New Screenwriter*, she told me how she once put a copy of her newest screenplay in the trunk of her car before attending a particular dinner party because she knew an important producer would be there. Indeed he was there, and indeed she gave him her screenplay. That is how Anna's *Masks* got made. It's a very good idea to keep an enveloped copy of your best screenplay in the trunk of your car at all times.

If you're having trouble getting your screenplay into the right hands, other routes into the marketplace exist. One of these routes is the screenwriting contest.

The good news about screenwriting contests is that, if they have industry recognition and if you win or are a finalist, in all likelihood an agent will want to read your work. The reason: It's pre-certified. The winner of a major screenwriting contest is likely to be sought after by aggressive young agents hoping to build their client rosters. Hungry new agents and hungry new screenwriters are made for each other.

The bad news is that most of these contests require an entry fee, usually about forty-five dollars. And some contests are merely moneymaking schemes for the contest sponsors. Be cautious before you send money. Check out the contest: Make some phone calls; see if they have a website. Screenwriters are raw meat for the thousands of sharks out there eager to make a dishonest buck. Be especially wary if a contest offers to "evaluate" your screenplay for a fee. My students' experiences with these types of contests have been horrendous. The "evaluations" usually turned out to be on the order of "nice try but it just doesn't quite fit our needs just now, but please send us a copy of your next screenplay." They may or may not mention that sending another screenplay costs another forty-five dollars. This kind of "evaluation" is a guarantee that you have come to the wrong place and are being hustled.

Caveat: Before you enter a contest, you should research it carefully. For example, one contest offers "representation by the Writers Guild of America." However, the Writers Guild is a union, not an agency. It does not solicit jobs for anyone. (You must be wary of this kind of contest hype.)

Some film schools offer screenplay contests, and their winners are publicized, gaining the immediate attention of agents. When I taught at UCLA, I would often recognize and chat with agents who were there to meet the winners at the awards ceremony. No doubt the same is true for other film schools of note.

Following is a short sampling of screenplay contests that I've been aware of for a number of years. These contests are often announced in *Written By* and other trade journals. (The contact information provided below is current as of the publication of this book. However, this information is subject to change at any time.) For a lengthier listing of screenplay contests, check out the MovieBytes website (www.moviebytes.com). Regularly updated listings can also be found in the Tennessee Screenwriting Association's monthly publication *Fade In* (www.tennscreen.com).

- American Cinema Foundation has an annual screenwriting competition in which an award is given "for excellence in screenplay writing which tells a positive story about specific fundamental values and their importance to society." The winner receives a substantial cash prize. American Cinema Foundation, 9911 W. Pico Blvd., Suite 510, Los Angeles, CA 90035; website: www.cinemafoundation.com.

- The Austin Heart of Film Screenplay Competition is a well-established contest. Austin Film Festival, 1600 Nueces, Austin, TX 78701; website: www.austinfilmfestival.org.

- The Humanitas Prize is a long-established contest. Its requirements are almost identical to those of the American Cinema Foundation. Humanitas' website: www.humanitasprize.org.

- New Century Writers Awards. First prize is a substantial cash award; cash awards also given for second through tenth place. New Century Awards, 32 Alfred St., Suite B, New Haven, CT 06512-3927; phone 203-469-8824; website: www.newcenturywriter.org.

- The Nicholl Fellowships in Screenwriting award up to five fellowships of $25,000 each (as of the date of this publication). Screenplays are judged by industry professionals. Nicholl Fellowships, Academy of Motion Picture Arts and Sciences, 8949 Wilshire Blvd., Beverly Hills, CA 90211-1972; website: www.oscars.org/nicholl.

- The Carl Sautter Memorial Scriptwriting Contest. To enter, you must be a member of the Scriptwriters Network. Scriptwriters Network, Carl Sautter Memorial Contest, 11684 Ventura Blvd., Suite 508, Studio City, CA 91604; website: www.scriptwritersnetwork.com.

- Screenplayoff awards a substantial cash prize for its contest's winner and cash prizes for the runner-up and semifinalists. Screenplayoff, P.O. Box 49370, Austin, TX 78765; phone 512-589-6480; website: www.screenplayoff.com.

- Screenwriting from the Soul Script Competition and American Screenwriters Association Competition. American Screenwriters Association, P.O. Box 12860, Cincinnati, OH 45212; website: www.asascreenwriters.com.

- Scriptapalooza awards prizes for the top three winners. Scriptapalooza, 7775 Sunset Blvd., PMB 200, Hollywood,

CA 90046; phone 323-654-5809; website: www. scriptapalooza.com.

- *scr(i)pt* magazine's Open Door Contest. scr(i)pt, 5638 Sweet Air Road, Baldwin, MD 21013; phone 410-592-3466; website: www.scriptmag.com.
- Tennessee Screenwriting Association Screenwriting Competition. Tennessee Screenwriting Association, P. O. Box 40194, Nashville, TN 37204-0194; website: www.tennscreen.com.
- The Walt Disney Studios/ABC-TV Fellowship Program offers up to eight yearlong salaried fellowships for working as a member of the Disney staff of writers. Fellowship Program Director, The Walt Disney Studios, 500 South Buena Vista St., Burbank, CA 91521-0705; phone 818-560-6894; website: www.members.tripod.com/~disfel.

The above are but a few from the plethora of screenwriting contests now available to you. I have no way of knowing how many of these contests will continue to exist annually, but based on the proliferation of such competitions, it's safe to say that there will be many screenwriting contests to enter for a long time to come. They appear to be an important avenue for getting screenplays read. They should not be overlooked. Entering multiple contests can be expensive, so I suggest that you choose your contests carefully. On the other hand, it will only cost you the price of a few phone calls to try to get an agent.

An important aside: Whenever you phone agents and/or submit screenplays to them, tell them of any contests in which your script has been a finalist or has won a prize. Be certain that you also mention such achievements in your all-important cover letters. The money you win in a screenwriting contest may be the least important aspect of winning. These contests are about recognition and the precertification that you are a better-than-average writer. Winning an important screenplay contest is a huge leg up.

If a legitimate contest's costs are affordable, by all means enter it. Choosing the contest that appears to be the most legitimate usually means finding the contest that offers the biggest prize, adding as a bonus a promise that your script will be read by an agent. If you study a contest's description and phone the outfit behind it, you should find it relatively easy to separate the important ones from the folk who are merely sifting the sea of screenplays with a small net, hoping to catch a whale. As with everything else in this business, do your homework, research, be wise, don't be taken for a sucker.

As the demand for new material grows, such creative visionaries as screenwriter-director Francis Ford Coppola are coming up with unusual and intriguing concepts. Coppola has a "virtual" studio on his American Zoetrope website (www.zoetrope.com). Here all sorts of writers can become part of the Zoetrope community—submit screenplays to his production company or short stories and one-act plays to his *Zoetrope All-Story* magazine. As Coppola was quoted in *Written By*: "I believe that there is an enormous untapped reservoir of writing talent. I'd guess that maybe forty people write all of the screenplays that Hollywood produces. I want those thousands of others to have a shot." Materials submitted to Zoetrope are read and evaluated by other writers. There is no cost for submitting material. In effect, you are giving Coppola a first look at your material. However, you are free to shop the same material around elsewhere, including seeking an agent or sending your screenplay out to contests, before Zoetrope makes a decision on whether they want it. This strikes me as a no-lose situation. (Coppola cautions all writers submitting material to first register whatever they're submitting with the WGA.)

I suggest you consider this route and similar nontraditional routes that may arise in the future simultaneously with your efforts to get an agent. You should be selling your work on all fronts. However, when all is said and done, there is no substitute for a direct connection with an agent. Agents are an integral aspect of the film industry. If they are seriously impressed with your work, they can help you create a career. I have had far more positive experiences with agents than negative ones, and a couple of agents have remained lifelong friends. Very few writers make it without an agent.

A Secret
Revolution

The best screenwriters in America were in a tricky situation. They were loyal members of the Writers Guild of America, west (which represents screenwriters living west of the Mississippi). And their guild had done a superb job in the past, winning a Minimum Basic Agreement for all writers of movies and television, extraordinary health and pension benefits, and the exclusive right for the guild to decide who deserves writing credit on any given screenplay or teleplay. But for a dozen years the guild had been essentially moribund, led by an executive director who some felt was too management friendly and officers who were too complacent and content with the status quo. WGA had become less a union and more a social club.

The screenwriters within the guild faced yet another problem—of their union's 9,000 members, the majority wrote primarily for television. And TV writers' interests are not identical to those of screenwriters. For the screenwriters, changes had to be made.

These changes began with casual conversations among a few of the most successful screenwriters in Hollywood: Frank Pierson (*Cool Hand Luke*), Callie Khouri (*Thelma and Louise*), Phil Robinson (*Field of Dreams*), and a few others. There was no plot, no organization, no grand scheme. They began to meet on Thursday evenings at one of their homes. Soon more screenwriting superstars—Ron Bass (*Rain Man*), Nicholas Kazan (*Reversal of Fortune*), Robert Towne (*Chinatown*), Scott Frank (*Out of Sight*), Eric Roth (*Forrest Gump*)—began to join these Thursday evening gatherings, where screenwriters discussed their work problems (e.g., being asked to do free rewrites, receiving delayed payments of the money owed them, not receiving recognition and respect, etc.).

These Thursday night meetings continued on an irregular basis, and the number of screenwriters attending them gradually increased. Remarkably, nobody spoke to the press or even to his or her own guild officials about these gatherings, which those involved agreed would remain secret.

Some of the attendees have reported that Robert Towne was the first to suggest that writers should get a percentage of the gross from the pictures they write. "Stars do, directors do, why not us?" For years, big-name producers, directors, and actors had been able to negotiate a percentage of the box-office gross from their picture's earnings, but no screenwriter had ever reportedly won it. Even these writers' agents scoffed at the idea. Hollywood's attitude toward screenwriters had not changed much since the '30s, when studio mogul Jack Warner called screenwriters "schmucks with typewriters."

But the writers who gathered on Thursday nights were a new breed of men and women with whom this condescending attitude did not sit well. They formed an exploratory group, began meeting with Columbia Pictures executives, and soon moved into serious negotiations with them.

On February 4, 1999, the industry awakened to a front-page story in the *New York Times* with the headline "Columbia Pictures to Share Movie Profits with Writers." It was a shock to everyone in the industry, including the Writers Guild. The achievement was revolutionary. But it was also vintage screenwriter behavior: In 1933, ten screenwriters met at the Knickerbocker Hotel in Hollywood to discuss their working conditions. They had all refused to join the studio's company union and, instead, eventually formed their own Screen Writers Guild, the precursor of the present Writers Guild of America, west.

All of the screenwriters from the Thursday night gatherings whom I have spoken to are reluctant to discuss anything other than the most general details of their little revolution. It's as if they had somehow been involved in a conspiracy, which is not the case. The truth is, they were doing what their own union leadership should have done but didn't during the years that the WGA was adrift with complacency.

In this book you will meet some of the key players in this quiet revolution. They are circumspect and surprisingly modest about their accomplishments. Possibly because, when the news broke, they were sniped at by fellow writers as being "elitist." Many of their fellow guild members did not seem to understand that all revolutions start with a few good men and women who open the gates for everyone. The truth is that more than 300 members of the guild are now eligible for this Columbia deal, as is any new writer selling his or her first screenplay for $750,000 or more—which is below the present going rate paid for screenplays for large Hollywood productions. It is forecast that, within a year, more than 500 screenwriters will be eligible for this deal. And gradually, kicking and screaming, the other studios will be forced to go along to remain competitive.

Bottom line: I think these genuine heroes (one of whom is a former twice-elected Writers Guild president) are embarrassed to have embarrassed their own union by doing what their leadership should have done long before. What the Thursday night group accomplished will have a direct bearing on the careers of all future Hollywood writers—of that you can be certain. In this book I am privileged to interview several of them, and I salute them all.

"I can only recall once when I sat down deliberately to write a film that was in a sense a polemic, and that was High Noon. . . . I started to do High Noon back in 1949 when the Un-American Activities Committee was just going into high gear in its Hollywood investigations, so called. . . . I could see this community beginning to crumble around the edges as these high-powered politicians came in accompanied by the headlines they were getting in the local press . . . putting this community through an inquisition that was getting more and more painful all the time for a lot of people. . . . And I could see that my time was coming. . . . I wanted to write about that. I wanted to write about what I considered the death of Hollywood. So that all shaped the writing of High Noon. That was very conscious. And that, incidentally, was a story of fear, because this was a community that was terribly afraid at that time. . . . You could almost smell the fear that rose— it was like the smog that we have now, you could see it."

—Carl Foreman, from *Word Into Image*
(courtesy of American Film Foundation)

A Powerful Director with a Powerful Vision

An Interview with

Richard Donner

"It's the words that count. A new screenwriter can get a million dollars for a screenplay."

—Richard Donner

Richard Donner began his career as an actor in the late Martin Ritt's television production of *Of Human Bondage*. Ritt suggested Donner become a director because, according to Donner, "I can't take direction." It was prescient advice. He became Ritt's assistant, working with Ritt and other directors during the halcyon days of live New York television drama. When television production moved from New York to Hollywood, Donner moved with it and soon found work directing the Steve McQueen TV series *Wanted: Dead or Alive*.

When I was beginning preproduction at MGM as the producer of a new NBC drama series, *Sam Benedict*, with a commitment of thirty-five one-hour episodes, Ben Conway, Donner's personable and determined agent, dropped by my office almost daily. He would merely stick his head in the door to shout, "Hire Dick Donner!" Conway's persistence paid off. I had Ben show me some Donner film. I liked what I saw and immediately booked him to direct one episode. It was among the better decisions I made during my twenty-five years as a television producer. When I saw Donner's first day's dailies, it was clear to me that this young director had a visual sense that was both original and exciting, far superior to any of the dozens of directors I had previously worked with in television, and his actors' performances were all crisp and concise. After he completed that first episode, I immediately booked him for as many episodes as our shooting schedule permitted.

Our working relationship soon developed into a warm, exuberant, and abiding friendship that remains vibrant to this day. Our collaboration continued through *Mr. Novak*, *Twilight Zone*, and *Gilligan's Island*. During our years working together on several popular network series, I was struck by Donner's ability to seize new ideas in a nanosecond and develop them far beyond my expectations. It was only a question of time until he found the vehicle that would bring him a big career in feature films. None of us who worked with him ever doubted that would happen.

Now—it seems almost suddenly—he has directed seventeen motion pictures, many of them international successes. Although his television work focused on dramas and comedies, he's became known for his action films (some of them a tad too violent for my taste).

After almost forty years of directing, his energy remains boundless; his big, booming voice and his youthful exuberance remain undiminished by age. A powerful creative force, Dick Donner is always in command of his set. His is a unique vision; nobody working in film today handles action sequences better (think of the chase sequences in the *Lethal Weapon* series, all of which he has directed). Could anyone shoot them with more excitement?

Donner is also that rarest of directors whose ego is not threatened by screenwriters. Indeed, he is among the very few who welcome writers on the set, never hesitating to ask them for their opinions and suggestions.

With a personality that is as rich and larger-than-life as his talent, Donner's bighearted generosity, kindness, and loyalty are legendary in the Hollywood community, where such qualities are rarer than sincerity. His practical jokes are also legendary, especially mid-shoot, where they break up the tension and stress of demanding production schedules. You can hear Dick Donner's big, booming laughter a block away (I know firsthand because, for years, I lived only a few blocks from him.)

Our conversation took place in the living room of the hillside house Donner shares with his wife, Lauren Shuler-Donner, high above the Sunset Strip. Donner's laughter frequently punctuated our interview as it has most of our conversations for the past thirty-nine years. It gives me great pleasure to introduce you to my dear friend, who is also a great director and, in more ways than one, a straight shooter.

FROUG: You have directed seventeen movies. The auteurists want to find a common thread or theme to these films. Is there one?

DONNER: Yes, there is a common thread: I enjoyed making every one of them. I make movies because I enjoy them.

FROUG: You make the movie you want to see?

DONNER: Exactly. I want to see it.

FROUG: Is there, for example, no common denominator between *The Omen* and *Superman* and *Inside Moves* and so forth?

DONNER: None whatsoever.

FROUG: Why do you choose a script?

DONNER: When I read a screenplay, if I'm captured by it, I "film" it as I read. So when I've completed the screenplay, I have seen the movie through my eyes, and that's terribly exciting. At that point, I become possessive and don't want someone else's vision, because if someone else makes the movie, I'll never have a chance to see it the way I already have. So, as simple or complicated as that is, that's how I make my decision. Almost every screenplay I read, unless it's truly that bad, I'll stick with it. If it has enough to keep me reading, then I see it.

FROUG: What keeps you reading?

DONNER: Many things. Why do you turn a page? Because what-ever is on the preceding page is so interesting that you have to find out what happens on the next page.

FROUG: How many pages will you give a writer before you give up on a script?

DONNER: I find myself very good to writers. Often I'll be reading a screenplay, and my wife, who as you know is an extremely talented, extraordinary producer, will ask about it. My response may be, "It's terrible." And her response will be, "So why are you reading it?" I'll say, "I don't know, I just have to finish it. Maybe something good will come out of it."

FROUG: You are the only person I know in this business who does that.

DONNER: That's true. Lauren will tell you that it's a rare occasion when I will walk out of a movie or not finish reading a screenplay. The thought that some person has actually spent hours, days, weeks, months, or even years to write gets me somehow emotion-ally committed to that person. So I read, always hoping there will be something good at the end of the rainbow.

FROUG: Looking back on all the movies you've directed, is there one you would single out as bad material—as a bad mistake that you made when choosing it?

DONNER: Yes. Probably a couple of them. I did them for different reasons.

FROUG: Financial being one of them?

DONNER: No, not really. Because my career took an incredible journey once I did *The Omen*.

"Why do you turn a page? Because whatever is on the preceding page is so interesting that you have to find out what happens on the next page."

FROUG: I remember when you showed me the *Omen* screenplay you said, "This is my ticket out of television."

DONNER: Exactly. And when I was making *The Omen*, I said, "I am going right back to television."

FROUG: Why?

DONNER: Because it was a very difficult shoot, and we did it for eleven dollars. That movie was brought in—with Gregory Peck and Lee Remick in London, Israel, and Italy—for two million dollars. It was so trying to make it that, at times, I just threw up my hands and said, "When this is over, I am going back to television, and I'm going to be very happy to be there."

FROUG: But you didn't, did you?

DONNER: No. I never went back.

FROUG: Well, you did *Tales from the Crypt*.

DONNER: I did go back on *Tales from the Crypt*.

FROUG: Why?

DONNER: I got involved with a producer who had a project that had been lying around for years—the *Tales from the Crypt* comic books. I remembered them well, and I thought, "Wow, this might be something fun to get involved with." So I put the money up for us to option it.

FROUG: Did it ring a bell for you, like *The Twilight Zone,* for example?

DONNER: Very much so. I was fortunate enough to do *The Twilight Zone* with a really wonderful producer. I forget his name at this point. No, I can't forget his name—it's William Froug. As a matter of fact, one of the *Twilight Zone*s I did was remade as part of *TZ: The Movie.* I am a living remade director.

FROUG: It was "Nightmare of 20,000 Feet." I didn't produce that one. My tenure began the day after you finished it. You shot all night; you ran way over budget. That entire season, CBS was on my case to get the series back on budget because of you.

DONNER: It wasn't my fault. MGM had to have the blue-screen sound stage the next day; I had to finish it. Stop blaming me, pal.

FROUG: How many readers has a screenplay gone through before it gets to you?

DONNER: It depends. Sometimes, if it's a personal connection or something that really sounds interesting to me, it comes to me right away.

FROUG: How did *The Omen* get to you?

DONNER: *The Omen* is an unusual story. It was originally called *The Antichrist.* It had been at every studio in town and had been rejected. It was at Warner Bros. at the time I received a call from an agent/ manager named Ed Rosen. He called me on a Friday and said, "There is a piece of material that is about to go into turnaround from Warner Bros. I think you should read it. I think there's something in it that others seem to be missing." And he sent it over.

FROUG: You had the weekend to make up your mind?

DONNER: It was brought to me on a Friday evening, and that evening I was going to dinner with Alan Ladd, Jr., and his then-wife, Patti. At the time, Alan was president of 20th Century-Fox. I picked up the script and started to read as I was getting dressed. Then there's a long dissolve because I couldn't put it down. I was two hours late for dinner, but I had realized in the reading that there was a hell of a good screenplay here and there was a good reason why it had not been made. It was an obvious horror—a demonic screenplay. There were terrible coincidences in someone's life, and you couldn't take the reality of the fact that there was a devil. It would be a good mystery/suspense thriller. So I ran to dinner, gave it to Alan Ladd, and said, "Please read this. I think it's sensational. It's going into turnaround at Warner on Monday." I owe it to his wife, who read it that weekend, driving to visit their child in camp. She read it as he drove. She said she loved it and made him read it coming back as she drove. He called me at eleven o'clock that night and said, "I think it's great. What would you do with it?" I said, "Eliminate the obvious. No cloven hooves, no devil gods, no covens. Just make it the worst moment in a man's life, one that could drive him insane enough that he could kill a child." He said, "I love it." Monday morning, I called the producers, Mace Neufeld and Harvey Bernhard, and I said, "I don't know if you remember me, but your picture is in turnaround today at Warner." They said, "Yeah, so what?" I said, "Well, I sold it to Fox." They said, "What are you talking about?" I said, "Fox is going to make it." The next day, Mace Neufeld went to Alan Ladd and said, "I'm thrilled that you're going to make this, but I've got a better director than Donner." Alan Ladd, who to my dying day I will love and respect, said, "Donner gave it to me. If he doesn't direct it, I won't make it." So that was *The Omen*.

FROUG: It was a huge hit. Does that kind of thing happen very often? You get a piece of material that you are hot for, give it to somebody, and suddenly you're off and shooting?

DONNER: We option material and, obviously, are very emotional about it. We show our excitement when we give it to the studios. Lots of times the studios don't see what we see. We have to fight and try to push it through. Then come rewrites. Some things get terribly overwritten. Too many writers, too many people involved, and the image of what we originally started out to make gets lost.

FROUG: That seems to be an increasing problem.

DONNER: It is, but I face this a lot less because I am not as involved as my wife, who is an active producer with many, many projects going. Studios are insecure in many ways; they are afraid to give a go on a project, and they have to impose themselves for some reason, probably to just guarantee their parking spot.

FROUG: What is the best movie you ever made?

DONNER: The best movie? That's like asking who your favorite kid is if you have children. Movies have emotionally different meanings for you, and your attachment to them is different. I have a great attachment to *The Omen* because it changed my life. I have a great emotional attachment to *Superman* because it set a standard and a pace and opened up an area of filmmaking that's gone on forever, because it brings a comic book to life. *Inside Moves* . . .

FROUG: That was a personal film?

DONNER: Very personal. I loved it. I did it for no money. Not only that, I put my own money into it just to get it made. We were mishandled by the domestic distribution company. It was terrible. Everyone dumped on it. They didn't know what to do with the picture. We came out at Christmas in tiny little theaters with no

"Some things get terribly overwritten. Too many writers, too many people involved, and the image of what we originally started out to make gets lost."

money, no marketing, no advertising, and we died. Yet it was the best-reviewed picture I ever did in my life. And it lives on to this day as somewhat of a cult film.

FROUG: Is *Inside Moves* your favorite?

DONNER: No, it's not. In a strange way, *Radio Flyer* is. It was a cult film for that time, and still is. Interestingly, *Radio Flyer* was a picture about child abuse, a very heavy piece, and we adhered to a great degree to the screenplay written by David Mickey Evans. We had the opportunity to change the end of the movie—to bring light into it and go beyond the reality of the pain of it. That would have been very commercial and probably would have done better at the box office. But that wasn't being honest to the piece, so we fought that and stayed with the screenplay.

FROUG: You don't regret it, obviously.

DONNER: Not at all. What I learned most about what a motion picture can do to and for an audience had to do with the making of *Radio Flyer*. Let me explain: We had many preview screenings and, of course, we got the overall audience reaction. But when a picture has this strong an emotional content, we utilize focus groups. We select twelve people from the audience and we sit down and have an upfront, in-your-face discussion of the film. Invariably, in every one of those screenings, there was someone in that group who said, "You know, I have never told anybody this, but I was an abused child." It brought tears to my eyes. It was almost giving them the opportunity to purge themselves. The picture was that important, that powerful. It carried a message. It still carries its message on video, and it makes me extremely proud. I don't know why it was made except by the good graces of Peter Guber of Columbia. Then and now, what executive would allow you to make a picture or run a TV spot that's about child abuse?

FROUG: These films have an eternal life. They still play on cable, and they will play forever.

DONNER: Forever. But the most important picture of my life was *Ladyhawke*.

FROUG: Where you met your wife?

DONNER: Yes. I met my wife, who was actually my producer, and who actually became my wife. My world turned around so beautifully that I will always hold *Ladyhawke* responsible for truly, truly changing my life for the better. And I love *Ladyhawke* because it was a beautiful story about unrequited love.

FROUG: After you finished *Lethal Weapon 3*, you said to me, "That's the end of that. Mel agrees, Danny agrees, no more *Lethals*." And then you went ahead and did *Lethal 4*. How did *4* do?

DONNER: Better than *1*, *2*, and *3*.

FROUG: Are you going for 5?

DONNER: I wasn't going for *2*, I wasn't going for *3*, and I wasn't going for *4*. As a matter of fact, in the original screenplay by Shane Black, the Mel Gibson character dies. I changed that, not because I looked at a franchise, I never thought of doing a *2*, but because I loved the character so much. He deserved to live, so we changed it. Will there be a *5*? I say no. Mel says no. Danny says no. But the studio says yes, and maybe, way down the line, I'll have an idea. That's the only way I make them—I get an idea and then I go to a writer.

FROUG: But this hasn't been the case for all the *Lethal*s.

DONNER: The only wall-to-wall script we had was on *LW 1*. But even that went through many changes. As we progressed to *2* to *3* to *4*, we would find ourselves up against the wall, having to shoot because of an availability of an actor or a delivery date demanded by the studio. So we would start with a not-quite-completed script, and we would spend almost every Saturday working on material for Monday's shoot. It was a nightmare, although a fun one.

FROUG: Writing as you were shooting?

DONNER: Yes. We'd spend those days writing. The production designer would be there with us, and as soon as we had what we thought were a few days' work, we'd send him off and he'd have to work Sunday to get ready for Monday. The making of the *Lethal Weapon* series has been extraordinary. It's been a career-raising experience for many of us: the actors, the above-the-line group, the below-the-line group, everyone, really. While not as expensive as the massive special-effects films—with computer graphics, etc.—it is a relatively expensive process now. When you do a series and the same people are part of it, their salaries go up, their percentage points of the profits go up. By the time you have four, five, six actors, and the writers and directors, it's hard for the studio to make a buck. If *5* comes up, and there is talk of it, I think I've got an answer. I've always wanted to do a very simple film, *A Day in the Life* . . . , starting from the moment Mel picks up Danny until the time they go to bed at night—separately, of course.

FROUG: It seems to me, from the first *Lethal* to the second, Mel became a little less crazy. He became a less neurotic, off-the-wall character than in the first one, where he seemed like he was really nuts.

DONNER: That's what I loved about it. I'd never done an action film, and I had been looking for an action film. Lauren and I read it. We couldn't put it down. I said, "I can't believe this. I've really found an action film that I want to make." The action wasn't gratuitous, there was a wonderful story, there was great character development, arc of character as we like to say, of a man who had no respect for life, much less his own, and he evolved in it. If you talk about character arc, this really was it. But I'm so tired of "character arc." Every writer, every acting coach, all they ever talk about is the arc and the character. But, in reality, that's just plain good writing without a predetermined definition. Here's a police officer who went from having no appreciation of life to having a tremendous desire to live in the end. That's just good writing.

The most wonderful thing I got out of making the first one was the great relationship Mel and Danny have with each other and the incredible, brilliant sense of humor they both have. Mel, especially, has a really far-out sense of humor—we call the things he says "Melisms," much like malaprops. He's probably one of the brightest people I've ever met in my life.

FROUG: I have heard again and again that the two of you are the two sides of the same coin.

DONNER: We talk in shorthand. For example, maybe the phone rings in the middle of a scene, so you say to an actor, "Hold the telephone." And a lot of actors say, "What do you mean?" I say, "Maybe it's your dentist and you have to have your teeth removed or your wife or your dog died or something."

FROUG: You're trying to get an attitude? Bring more energy to a scene?

DONNER: Something that's going to give another dimension to that scene and that character. With Mel Gibson, you say, "Hey, the telephone." And he says, "Leave me alone; I got it." He runs with it brilliantly. So we talk in shorthand.

FROUG: And the chemistry is both onscreen and off, I'm told.

DONNER: It is a delight to make these films. It is a joyous occasion for sixty-eight or seventy days. You dread the last day of photography because it is a wonderful thing.

FROUG: I'm told that the *Lethal Weapon* series has grossed over half a billion dollars.

DONNER: More than that.

FROUG: More than that? It must be the most successful buddy movie series in history.

DONNER: I think it is. Oh, by far.

FROUG: Now you've got a new movie cooking. Tell me a little about that.

DONNER: Well, I hate to talk about it.

FROUG: I know you don't want to, but I talked with the writer, Brian Helgeland, and he said it was a Western about this character that seized you and seized him.

DONNER: Well, there is a great backstory to this piece. Many years ago, when I was directing television, I would shoot pilots or redo pilots, like *The Wild, Wild West*, for a lot of producers. In those days, I would walk away with a royalty of maybe $150. That was it. So I said I wanted to do a Western of my own. I decided to do a series on a derivation of the names of western towns, which have these wonderful names: Broken Knee, Wounded Knee, Virgin Fall, etc. So as I researched the derivations of all these towns, I came to a county in Texas called Deaf Smith. I said, "Oh, my God, what is this?" So I spent a lot of time researching this county, which, it turned out, was named for this wonderful man, a gunfighter, an Indian guide, a scout. He was with Sam Houston at the Battle of San Jacinto. I fell in love with the character. I decided to make a motion picture about Deaf Smith, so I wrote a twenty-five-page treatment of the character.

I have a dear friend named Paul Heller, who recently produced a movie called *David and Lisa* [1998 television movie]. At the time, 1959, he had just come back from Europe, where he had met James Jones, who wanted to write a Western. Paul asked me, "Do you have a Western?" "Do I have a Western?!" So I went to Paris and lived with James Jones for close to three months. But I realized the moment I got started with him I was going to have major problems, because I had a character in search of a story and he wanted to change the character, and the story wasn't evolving. In any event, I was very upset with the end result, and it stayed on his desk. Finally it reverted back to me.

FROUG: You never forgot that character?

DONNER: Forty years I have carried this character and the story.

FROUG: So you met Brian, and you talked about Deaf Smith?

DONNER: I met many, many, many great, wonderful writers, and I would talk to them. But nobody could find it. Nobody could hit it.

I was doing a picture for Warner Bros. called *Assassins*, with Stallone and Antonio Banderas. It was a picture that was done for money, but I think it was a good picture, and it was the best Stallone. I needed someone to rewrite it, and Brian Helgeland came on to do that. I fell in love with him as a person. I told him the Deaf Smith story. We talked about it on and off before he wrote *Conspiracy Theory*, which turned out very well. We stayed close, and we talked about it again. Then, one day not too long ago, Brian walked into my office and said, "Read this." It was eleven pages, and it was my Western. It was everything I wanted. The storyline was brilliant. He captured it to a T—better than I ever thought I could.

FROUG: So at that point you made a deal?

DONNER: Well, here is the deal I made with him: I shook his hand and I said, "Do you want some money to write this?" He said, "No." He wrote it. I love it. And he'll produce it with me. He'll be there as writer and as co-producer.

FROUG: What will you do with it?

DONNER: My intentions are, with one more little polish, to go to a major actor and give him the screenplay with the backstory.

FROUG: Is that the element that will make it go?

DONNER: I think it will go without it, but I would like to make it a package, so that I could walk into a studio and say that I have so-and-so and the screenplay. Here is the budget. Here is the schedule. Here is the entire package. And I don't think anybody is going to say no.

FROUG: Do you have a producer in mind?

DONNER: I know what you're driving at, Bill. My wife is a producer. Lauren and I have over thirteen years of marriage, sixteen years of being together, a few movies under our belt. She has made a lot more movies than I have during the period of our marriage. But we decided that it's best that we live and love but don't work together, so that it doesn't affect living and loving. After all, I am a temperamental old codger, and movies bring such a weight and burden. I tend to carry them around and let them get to me too much. I think we are smart not to let work affect our personal life. What I have in my marriage is far superior to any motion picture I have ever made.

FROUG: What is the market like today for screenwriters?

DONNER: It couldn't be better. It's the words that count. A new screenwriter can get a million dollars for a screenplay.

FILMOGRAPHY

1961	*X-15*, director
1968	*Salt and Pepper*, director
1970	*Lola* (a.k.a. *Twinky*), director
1976	*The Omen*, director
1978	*Superman*, director
1980	*Inside Moves*, director
1981	*The Final Conflict*, executive producer
1982	*The Toy*, director

1985	*Ladyhawke*, director and producer (with Lauren Shuler)
1985	*The Goonies*, director and producer
1987	*Lethal Weapon*, director and producer (with Joel Silver)
1988	*Scrooged*, director and producer (with Art Linson)
1989	*Lethal Weapon 2*, director and producer (with Joel Silver)
1989	*Tales from the Crypt*, executive producer (with David Giler, Walter Hill, Joel Silver, Robert Zemeckis)
1991	*Delirious*, executive producer
1991	*Radio Flyer*, director and producer
1992	*Lethal Weapon 3*, director and producer
1993	*Free Willy*, executive producer (with Arnon Milchan)
1994	*Maverick*, director and producer (with Bruce Davey)
1995	*Free Willy 2*, executive producer (with Arnon Milchan)
1994	*Assassins*, director and producer
1997	*Free Willy 3*, executive producer (with Arnon Milchan)
1997	*Conspiracy Theory*, director and producer (with Joel Silver)
1998	*Lethal Weapon 4*, director and producer
1999	*Any Given Sunday*, executive producer

The Hit Maker

An Interview with

Lauren Shuler-Donner

"I see setting up the conflicts, escalating the conflicts, and resolving them. But I also learned a long, long time ago about 'plot need': Will Dorothy get home? Will Bogart get Bergman? What is Rosebud? It is why you sit in your seat, and, for me, it is the question that the character always asks. What does the character want? What is the conflict? To me, that is ultimately how it breaks down into those three acts."

—Lauren Shuler-Donner

Lauren Shuler-Donner is among the most prolific and successful producers in the recent history of American motion pictures. The majority of her nineteen movies have enjoyed box-office success. If she were a baseball player, she'd be batting around .800. And she's done it the hard way: While most producers are busy assaulting us with volumes of vulgarity and violence, Shuler-Donner has chosen to make PG-rated movies suitable for the entire family. And they are not of the dumb-and-dumber variety. Her films have a degree of sophistication and intelligence. In spite of or perhaps because of their PG ratings, several of her movies have gone for grand-slam home runs. Her latest since our interview was completed is *Any Given Sunday*, a Donner Company production that opened to good reviews and a number one at the box office.

Shuler-Donner's husband, Richard Donner, describes his wife as a "workaholic," which seems self-evident in the quantity of her film output. But forget any preconceived notions you might have of how a high-powered Hollywood producer looks or behaves. You would never recognize the dynamo who is responsible for this extraordinary productivity. Ms. Shuler-Donner is a soft-spoken, attractive, understated woman. Wearing her chic, sophisticated attire, she radiates a quiet self-assurance without a trace of arrogance or bravado. Yet one can sense her strength and authority. Shuler-Donner is not someone you would want to mess with; she will outsmart you before the umpire tosses out the first ball.

FROUG: According to my score sheet, you have produced seventeen movies, and almost all of them have been hits. Do you have a common thread to your movies?

SHULER: I'm not sure that there is a common thread. They all have some comedy in them. They have a lot of heart, and they are all entertaining. Hopefully, they're intelligent. Hopefully, they all have something to say. I lean toward comedy, especially romantic comedy, but I'm drawn to movies with a strong theme, a message subtly woven through.

FROUG: Is comedy the hardest thing to do?

SHULER: The hardest because, if it's not funny, you're dead in the water. And it's not easy to be funny. If a part of a dramatic story doesn't work, then fine, the overall story probably works. But if people don't laugh at a comedy, they're disappointed and you have a flop.

FROUG: How do you know if it's funny?

SHULER: If I laugh out loud while I'm reading the script.

FROUG: Does that ever happen?

SHULER: Oh, my gosh, yes. Absolutely. Then it's funny again when you are casting and when you are shooting and, hopefully, while you're editing. But the true test is watching and listening to your audience.

FROUG: How many readers has a script gone through before you read it?

SHULER: It depends. It depends on who sent the script, and it depends on who is the writer. If the script came from an agency, then somebody in our company reads it.

FROUG: Suppose it is an unknown writer, let's call him Joe Smith.

SHULER: Joe Smith sends it in. Then the reader covers it.

FROUG: The cover is a synopsis?

SHULER: Yes.

FROUG: And an opinion?

SHULER: And an opinion. And if it's a positive opinion or if it is even a medium-to-positive opinion, then somebody in our company, Julie Durk or Michael Aguilar, will read it. If they like it, then I read it.

FROUG: So it has been through at least two readers?

SHULER: Exactly. One reader and one development person.

FROUG: What's the difference between a reader and a development person?

SHULER: Our development person is someone whose taste I trust very much. Their taste is similar to ours. Or, if it's not, then it's younger or darker, but it has to be something to which we respond. A development person also works with writers, the studio, and the director. They'll often receive some sort of executive producer, co-producer, or producer credit for their work.

FROUG: What does one do to become a development person? What if somebody reads this book and says, "I have a strong background in film but can't make it through this iron gate of Hollywood as a screenwriter? How do I become a development person?"

SHULER: Before we hire development people, I put them through the wringer. I find out what they've done before, whom they've

"Before we hire development people, I put them through the wringer."

worked for before. I ask them their favorite movies. I see if we are on the same wavelength, if we like the same movies. I meet with them personally to find out what they're like. My movies are all PG-13. And the person I hire has to have to a certain taste and an intelligence and be well read. And I want them hungry— I want them to want my job. Literally, I want them to be assertive, confident in their story instincts.

FROUG: Do you find many qualified people?

SHULER: No, but it is always very obvious who is right for the job. You sense who gets it and who doesn't.

FROUG: So Joe Smith has gotten his script through the reader and your development person, and now it's on your desk. Do you work directly with the writer?

SHULER: Yes.

FROUG: In what sense? Do you sit down and go page by page or do you discuss it?

SHULER: We discuss what needs to be fixed in the script in general: story, structure, fleshing out the characters. Then, when everyone is clear, we go page by page. Sometimes we do a page one rewrite before we turn the script in to the studio. The first draft makes an indelible impression, so we try to put our best foot forward.

I work with writers in many different ways. One would be a spec script that I want an option on. Recently a spec script came into the company. The development executive, Michael, read it and loved it. He kept pushing me to read it. I read it. I loved it. I called the agent and told him I loved it. I called the writer and told him it was great but it needed a bit of work. There were a few things wrong: The main character in the first half of the script was so unlikable that he was unredeemable. And the love story was too much of a surprise. It wasn't laid in. It wasn't set up right. So I asked the writer to make those few changes. He made them, and now we are out to an actor. We are packaging it, and I'll take it out to a studio.

FROUG: Please explain "packaging."

SHULER: Packaging is bringing on a desirable "element," i.e., an actor or a director. First and foremost, choose the right director for the movie—a director who shares your vision of the story. Secondly, choose a director whom the studio wants to be in business with. It's the same for an actor: If you're going to attach them early on, they need to have a box-office cachet. I prefer bringing on a director first, and then choosing the actor together.

I am nonexclusive to Warner Bros., which means that I must submit all materials for their consideration first. If they turn down a project, I may take it elsewhere. If another studio offers me a movie, I can also produce for them. All studios welcome PG movies. *You've Got Mail* was PG. PG doesn't necessarily mean juvenile films anymore.

Another way we develop material is to take an idea like *X-Men*, which has been a comic book for thirty-five years, and turn it into a movie. We sought a writer who could take this concept and turn it into a movie. Other than that, we were pretty open. Each writer came in and pitched their idea.

FROUG: Has the writer been paid any money at this point?

SHULER: No, not at that point.

FROUG: He is doing this on spec?

SHULER: He is doing it on spec. I cannot hire a writer without hearing their ideas.

Here was an interesting situation: I had a movie called *The Death and Life of Bobby Z* at Warner Bros. It was a very hot book. We did a preempted bid with Warner Bros., which means Warner Bros. took it off the market. I went directly to a writer, Henry Bean, a fabulous writer who wrote *Internal Affairs*, among other things. He had tons of credits. Henry liked the book. We wanted to fly him out. But Henry wanted to outline the script first, for himself, so that he could see if he could adapt the book. He told us that, if we liked his "take" on the book, then we could fly him out. The outline was perfect. I loved it. Warner read it and loved it. We flew Henry out and just fine-tuned the details. He went on to write an incredible script.

FROUG: Did he receive any money up to then?

SHULER: No.

FROUG: When does the writer get any money?

SHULER: Once we are going to enter development, or once we option their spec script.

FROUG: What's the percentage of the screenplays that you get that you like that actually get made into films?

SHULER: Twenty percent. Thirty percent if we're lucky.

FROUG: That's a pretty big percentage, isn't it?

SHULER: It's normal. We home-grow almost all of our movies. We develop more screenplays than we buy spec scripts and books. It just works that way. It's interesting, I was at Motown when I first started out. Because we were Motown, we hardly got any material. So my training was to either come up with ideas myself or to establish relationships with writers that were so strong that the writers would bring me movies. So that's how I learned about development.

FROUG: What budget do you aim for these days?

SHULER: Each movie is different. The script tells you how much it will cost. The big expenses are big-name stars, visual effects, location costs, and children.

FROUG: *You've Got Mail* must have had a huge budget because you had Tom Hanks and Meg Ryan.

SHULER: It was huge above the line. But, because of that, it wasn't huge below the line. We kept costs down by shooting on locations in New York, so that wasn't bad.

FROUG: Did you say to yourself, "Those stars were very good in *Sleepless in Seattle*. I want to build a story around them"?

SHULER: No, no. It started with the movie *Shop Around the Corner*, part of the Turner library which we were looking at. Actually, Julie Durk, who is one of my development people, saw the movie and told me about it. Her job is to bring in movies. I took a look at it and loved it. It was very old-fashioned. This was in 1993, and I had just gone online on the Internet, and because of that, I figured out how to update the movie. Then we went to Turner. We told them that they had this great movie, *Shop Around the Corner*. We explained how to update it, using the Internet, e-mail, etc., until the characters meet. Turner agreed. Then we went to Nora [Ephron] and she agreed to develop it. Nora and her sister, Delia, wrote the script.

FROUG:　How many years did you spend with it?

SHULER:　Well, Nora was just setting up *Michael*, the movie with John Travolta. Once she finished that movie, she owed Columbia a script with Delia, *Hanging Up*, which they are just filming now with Meg Ryan and Lisa Kudrow, with Diane Keaton directing. Once she and Delia finished that, then they finally were free to write our script, almost three years later. But Nora had planned to direct a beautiful script she had written previously. Fortunately, Tom Hanks agreed to star in *You've Got Mail*, and everyone agreed to make that movie first.

FROUG:　The picture did big business, yes?

SHULER:　It was huge.

FROUG:　What is your favorite of the movies you've produced?

SHULER:　That's hard to say. You love them all. I am really prone to romantic comedies, so I am prone to *You've Got Mail* and *Dave*. Those are my two favorites. And *Ladyhawke*, because it gave me the opportunity to fall in love with my husband.

FROUG:　Where did you get the idea for *Free Willy*?

SHULER:　An actor, Keith Walker, gave the script to Dick. He had had the script for a long, long time, and he was trying to get it made. It was a lot sappier and cornier than the movie we ultimately made. I got involved, and I said we have to toughen it up. Originally, Jason Richter's character was a deaf-mute orphan who lived with nuns. He didn't speak until the end of the movie when he released the whale.

FROUG:　It was all hearts and flowers?

SHULER:　Saccharin. My idea was for him to be a juvenile delinquent, and to make it edgy, hipper. We brought in another writer—two writers, actually.

FROUG: Is it a frequent or usual occurrence that, after you get a project going, you have to bring in a second writer to rewrite the first writer?

SHULER: It depends. My feeling is that a lot of people call themselves writers, but only a handful of people really are writers. When you have Nora and Delia Ephron write the script, or Gary Roth writing *Dave*, there is no need to bring in another writer. John Hughes writing *Mr. Mom* or Joel Schumacher writing *St. Elmo's Fire*—fine, those are all writers. However, in some cases you have people who have had a wonderful idea but cannot carry it to fruition.

"My feeling is that a lot of people call themselves writers, but only a handful of people really are writers."

FROUG: How many really terrific writers do you run across?

SHULER: Few.

FROUG: And they are getting big money now, aren't they?

SHULER: Yes. Good writers deserve every single penny.

FROUG: Do you see most screenplays following a three-act paradigm?

SHULER: I do, actually. I see setting up the conflicts, escalating the conflicts, and resolving them. But I also learned a long, long time ago about "plot need": Will Dorothy get home? Will Bogart get Bergman? What is Rosebud? It is why you sit in your seat, and, for me, it is the question that the character always asks. What does the character want? What is the conflict? To me, that is ultimately how it breaks down into those three acts. And that is what keeps you in your seat. You want to find out if the character will get what they need or what they want.

FROUG: Does the character have to be likable?

SHULER: Not necessarily in the beginning, as long as they end up likable. But there are always exceptions. It depends on the movie. In *Unforgiven*, Clint Eastwood's character was not likable.

FROUG: Two of your most successful movies were written by second-generation screenwriters: *Dave* was written by the son of screenwriter Arthur Ross. You've also worked with the Ephrons, children of Henry and Phoebe Ephron, who were great screen-writers. Do you often see this family history of screenwriters?

SHULER: Yes, absolutely. We see it a lot.

FROUG: If I am a new writer, what's the best way for me to get a script to you?

SHULER: You call our company, and they give you a release form. You sign the release form, and then you send it with your script.

FROUG: Will you read a script if doesn't come from an agent?

SHULER: No. But readers in our company will. And they know our taste, so if there is any sort of a general liking about it, even if the readers don't like the script but they like the writing, it goes up to the head of our development.

FILMOGRAPHY

1976   *ABC's Wide World of Entertainment*, associate producer
1977   *Thank God It's Friday*, associate producer
1978   *Amateur Night at the Dixie Bar & Grill*, producer

1983	*Mr. Mom*, producer (with Lynn Loring)
1985	*Ladyhawke*, producer (with Richard Donner)
1985	*St. Elmo's Fire*, producer
1986	*Pretty in Pink*, producer
1988	*Three Fugitives*, producer
1991	*Radio Flyer*, producer
1991	*The Favor*, producer
1993	*Dave*, producer
1993	*Free Willy*, producer (with Jennie Lew Tugend)
1995	*Free Willy 2*, producer (with Jennie Lew Tugend)
1995	*Assassins*, executive producer (with Dino De Laurentiis)
1997	*Free Willy 3*, executive producer
1997	*Volcano*, executive producer
1998	*Bulworth*, executive producer
1998	*You've Got Mail*, producer (with Nora Ephron)
1999	*Any Given Sunday*, producer
2000	*X-Men*, producer

"Writing is no trouble; you just jot down ideas as they occur to you. The jotting down is simplicity itself—it's the occurring which is difficult."
— Stephen Leacock

"No writer I know knows literally what he is going to write until the first stumbling scenes of the first act have been written and his characters have begun to assume a physical reality to him. I have never written an outline that retained its rigid structure all the way into the final draft. Scenes that I reckoned to be eight pages in length turn out to be six lines of dialogue, and scenes I never conceived suddenly demand to be written. Most writers count on the impetus of their dialogue to disgorge new lines of dramatic movement, new insights into their characters, and even a new tone or flavor to the overall script. Outlines do serve a vital function for the writer in that they keep him from plunging into the actual writing before he has thought out a general line for his story. . . ."
— Paddy Chayefsky, *Television Plays*

"No passion in the world is equal to the passion to alter someone else's draft."
— H. G. Wells

Spinning on a Paradigm

In 1979, Professor Syd Field published his now-famous book *Screenplay*. In it he told us that, as head of the story department at Cinemobile Systems, he spent two years reading screenplays submitted to his company for possible production. During his time in that job, he estimates that he read and synopsized more than 2,000 screenplays. Out of these, he found only forty that he could recommend.

Based upon these readings, he concluded that every screenplay could be broken down into three acts, and that all screenplays contain this basic linear structure. In addition, he informed us that all screenplays contain what he calls a "paradigm": Act one ends with a "plot point" occurring between pages 25 and 27, and act two ends with a "plot point" occurring between pages 85 and 90. Field claims that in all screenplays "the paradigm holds firm."

Field's paradigm is an interesting observation, but in the long run it's a disservice to screenwriters. My firsthand experience, reading far more than 2,000 screenplays and working with and knowing scores of top-ranked screenwriters, teaches me a different lesson: The more talented the screenwriter, the less likely he or she is to follow Field's paradigm, or anybody's paradigm.

The fundamental truth is that Field's paradigm is not valid for every screenplay. Another unavoidable fact is that not all screenplays are structured in three acts. *Citizen Kane*? (Come on, Syd, give us a break!) In *Kane*, which is the precursor of many modern screenplays, there's a "plot point" coming at you every three or four pages. Herman Mankiewicz improvised the screenplay, dictating it to his secretary. (Orson Welles' name is on the screenplay only because his RKO contract required that he receive a writing credit.)

Nonetheless, many screenwriters and screenwriting teachers jumped on the paradigm bandwagon when it appeared. I had a brief flirtation with it myself until I began to read the screenplays that resulted from following its rigid formula. (I've also heard fellow professionals in the industry complain again and again about the formulaic nature of so many of the screenplays they see.)

Let's examine the root of Field's paradigm. Cinemobile, Field's employer, was a unique, successful, and highly respected mobile production-equipment facility, which basically did a splendid job of delivering filmmaking equipment to filmmaking locations. But Cinemobile's founder decided to expand his operation to include producing his own films. He recruited financial partners and hired Field as the head of his story department, hoping to discover screenplays that could help build a viable studio. However, one of the problems Cinemobile faced was that agents and big-name screenwriters did not rush to submit their best screenplays to this new player. Hollywood's "old boys club" has never welcomed competition. The big boys always outbid newcomers for properties, and they always make certain that they get first look at the best screenplays. What is left over goes to the small independents, and Cinemobile, when it began producing films, was among the newest and smallest of the independents.

In his job, Field read whatever screenplays came his way. In all likelihood, the majority of the 2,000 screenplays submitted to Cinemobile were not top-of-the-line work from established screenwriters.

My educated guess is that, through no fault of his own, what often got to Field were rejects from the majors and big-name directors and stars. (No wonder that he found only forty of the 2,000 worth recommending.) Yet out of this 2,000 he formulated his paradigm. So you might ask yourself if these are the models upon which you want to base your screenplay.

The paradigm theory was an interesting tool for study but never a road map for writing an original screenplay. For those of you who want to move forward and make a breakthrough in your work, I urge you to find your own style, develop your own structure—be creative. Following the herd has never been the road to an outstanding career.

What appears evident when looking at movies made by the best of the new generation of screenwriters is that the paradigm has outlived its usefulness. if it ever had any. Today it is as outmoded as the Twist. Times change, especially in popular art, and what is the most popular art on the planet? The movies! Modern screenwriters are constantly redefining structure with dazzling effect.

Making Your Move

If you have completed two or three polished final-draft screenplays, have received positive feedback on them from objective professional screenwriters or aspiring screenwriter friends, have perhaps entered a screenwriting contest or two, and have been working on getting an agent, you are now poised to go for a motion-picture career. And you have properties!

Does anybody not know the three rules for selling property? (1) location, (2) location, and (3) location. Without a doubt, that location is Los Angeles. (Very few screenwriters have made it into the mainstream without moving to L.A.) Therefore, the best and fastest way to build your screenwriting career is to move to Los Angeles, where you will be able to establish vital contacts, meet fellow writers, and build a support network. Getting started is never easy; attempting to do so from a distance is extremely difficult.

Your first order of business is to contact anyone you know in L.A. who knows anyone who works in "the business." Let them know of your plans. You'll need all the relocation advice you can get.

For a month before you leave, you might want to subscribe to *Daily Variety*, *Weekly Variety*, or the *Hollywood Reporter*. These Hollywood trade journals report what's shooting where, what's being planned, and what TV shows are in production. Be warned: Along with the legit hard facts, you will also find a lot of public-relations production announcements that have less substance than cotton candy.

Long before you make a date for your move, write to the UCLA Extension Writers' Program, 10995 LeConte Ave., #440, Los Angeles, CA 90024-2883; phone 310-825-0415 or 800-388-UCLA; e-mail: writers@unex.ucla.edu. Request their catalog of writing courses as well as their most recent Writers' Program quarterly. After you have received their quarterly, time your move to allow you to enroll in the courses of your choice. Even better, try to schedule your move to coincide with their annual four-day Los Angeles Writers' Conference.

No institution in the world offers a more comprehensive and diverse schedule of screenwriting courses than UCLA Extension. Be selective; these courses are expensive, but they could turn out to be your best career investment. Learning more about screenwriting and getting professional feedback on your work is reason enough to enroll in a UCLA screenwriting course. An equally compelling reason is that, in these classes, you will meet and befriend fellow aspiring screenwriters as well as some professionals who are trying to improve their work. You will also meet teachers who are professional screenwriters and professionals who have been invited to class as guest speakers. Make it a point to develop relationships with your teachers and the other professionals. You want them to know you; you want to stand out from the crowd. This is where your networking will begin. Nothing, aside from your talent as a screenwriter, is more important in building your career than networking with industry professionals. This networking might lead you to job opportunities, introductions to agents, suggestions about how to get your career started, etc.

Getting into the Writers Guild of America is one of the best things that can happen to your career. (Remember, you don't have to sell a script to get into the guild; you merely have to have a contract to write a script.) The benefits of WGA membership are so numerous and bountiful that only an imbecile would not join if qualified. I have been a member of WGA for fifty-two years and have served on its board and many of its committees. I have been named a Lifetime Member. Trust me, I am biased.

Membership in WGA does not guarantee you a job (in any given week, perhaps 1,000 of the 9,000 members of WGA may be unemployed), but it gives you a platform of professional status upon which to build and enhance your career. As a member, you will receive *Written By*, the guild's monthly magazine (you don't have to be a member to subscribe), and you will also receive *Member News* (for members only), in which you will discover a fund of information that is as beneficial as it is wide-ranging. Until you do make it into WGA, get a friend to loan you a copy of *Member News*. Aside from its list of member-only events, it also lists interesting events open to all writers.

As soon as you are settled in Los Angeles, apply for a job at every studio (whether you need the money or not). Apply for any job—secretarial assistant to anyone on the lot, tour guide, reader, flunky, or "gofer." (Gofers often get their screenplays read.) Do what so many of your fellow menial workers do: Write screenplays at night and on weekends. You will be surprised how many office workers, messengers, support-staff members, secretaries, et al. are closet screenwriters.

Being there, inside the gates, is the single best way to launch your career. Once you are working on a lot, you are immediately part of the brotherhood (or sisterhood) of the motion-picture industry. You have instantly moved from outsider to insider, which makes a world of difference. If you have any people skills whatsoever, you will quickly make friends, be welcomed into the "family," and casually meet the important folk you want to meet, most of whom you will find to be cordial and friendly because you are now one of them.

Agents crisscross studio lots servicing clients. You will quickly learn who they are and what agencies they are with. Strike up brief, casual conversations with them, but do not hand them your screenplay unless you have their permission to do so.

Many stars, star directors, and big-time producers enjoy helping the new people on the block. The reason for this may be simply that all of them have been where you are now. As you get to know these people and move up to working in their offices, they will gain confidence in you, and you will gain ease in your ability to sell yourself and your work.

However, all the schmoozing in the world will not sell your screenplay. Every writer in recorded history had to make his or her mark exactly the same way you will have to: one word at a time. I wish you the best of luck as I point out that hardworking, dedicated, determined writers create their own luck.

Panic Hollywood

Today, the payoff for a blockbuster movie is well over one hundred million dollars. (Grosses for 1999 were higher than they'd been in forty years.) Which is why a few superstar screenwriters are paid as much as $250,000 per week to rewrite, or "rescue," screenplays that often have been written by other superstar screenwriters. Mind you, there may be nothing actually wrong with the particular screenplay that's being "rescued," but with a lot of careers on the line and as much as sixty to one hundred million dollars committed to a production, there is an understandable tendency for execs, producers, stars, and directors to push the panic button—the rewrite button.

Such is the insanity of this rewrite panic that a group of the industry's most prestigious screenwriters recently held a Writers Guild panel discussion to address it. Ron Bass, Aaron Sorkin, Callie Khouri, Tom Shulman, et al. talked about the harm done to their profession and to their reputations when they are called in to rewrite one another. Rewriting is a thankless job (but the money is usually irresistible). Eric Roth once remarked to me, "How much can you actually improve a screenplay in two or three weeks of rewriting? And often there's nothing wrong with them," he added.

How does this current state of madness affect *you*? In panicky situations, studio execs turn to a handful of the top professionals, but when these star screenwriters turn them down (which is not a rare occurrence), the execs begin checking with agents for the availability of their very best young writers, including new writing talent. If you've written a screenplay that is exceptionally good, it very well might circulate around town, and your talent might be noted for future assignments, even though nobody may ever produce the particular screenplay that's circulating. In which case *you* just might be the new writing talent that is called in to feed the rewrite panic.

Several of my gifted UCLA students have made handsome livings from rewrites, without ever having had an original screenplay produced. For these younger writers, $60,000 a week is not an unheard-of salary. One of my students was hired to do a rewrite and stayed on for *six months* at that salary—even though not a word of what he wrote ever reached the screen! Several of my students feed off the rewrite chain without ever receiving screen credit. It is certainly not what they had in mind for their screenwriting careers, but who can knock the money?

Hollywood is a town of many panics. Another panic that's always in play is How do we feed the distribution chain? How do we get enough pictures to the theaters? So, like divers scouring the ocean floors for buried treasures, young, overeducated, underexperienced studio executives desperately search for screenplays that will secure their jobs and make them major players in Movietown.

Supply and demand is the key to every marketplace, and today, as never before, the demand for good screenwriters far exceeds the supply. Note the qualifier "good." Nobody will knowingly buy crap, no matter how desperate they are. Hack writing may make you a living, but it won't win you respect or put you in demand. ("He's an okay writer" isn't a compliment in Hollywood.)

Obviously your life will be much easier and more profitable if you are among the great screenwriters. But the odds are that you are not. Are you wasting your time? Are you unemployable? Certainly not. Write the best screenplays you can write. But if you're not Paddy Chayefsky, you can still do quite well for yourself. Both the big screen and the small screen must settle for the best they can get in a time of need, and that time of need is constant.

When the panic buttons are pushed in Hollywood, the words most likely to come out are "Get me a writer!" A good story, well dramatized, can be your ticket into a new world. Panic Hollywood will work for you.

"Screenplays are not dialogue. Screenplays are structure; that's all they are. They are basic. . . . Certainly dialogue is helpful, certainly literate dialogue is pleasant, certainly funny dialogue is fun . . . but the reality is, the reason we can't quote many lines of dialogue, besides "Frankly, my dear, I don't give a damn," is because the dialogue doesn't matter that much. Obviously good dialogue is better than inept dialogue at any time, but for the most part, you have to have the scene that is in its proper place in the structure of the piece."
— William Goldman, from *Word Into Image*
(courtesy of American Film Foundation)

Leaving Large Fingerprints

An Interview with

Nicholas Kazan

"If you learn to write by following a certain paradigm, you do everything the way everyone else does; your screenplay looks like everyone else's. It just blends into an endless stream of similar pieces of work."

—Nicholas Kazan

When I first saw *Reversal of Fortune*, I knew at once that I had to interview the author of that extraordinarily creative and intricate screenplay. I was excited by the fresh and idiosyncratic style of the work and by the obvious challenge the screenwriter faced: How do you turn the appeal of a verdict (not a trial, which is easy) into an exciting drama? Kazan did it with aplomb and originality. It was another case of a writer who ignored conventional wisdom (the three-act paradigm) and opted to go his own way. No surprise that it won him an Academy Award nomination. I urge you to study this movie and, specifically, the screenplay as you view it. It is the work of a master. When Nick Kazan is on his game, nobody is better.

Kazan began writing plays as a student at the University of California, Berkeley. They were performed in local theaters, earning him recognition and a Hollywood agent who agreed to make him a "back-pocket" client, meaning that he would do very little for the young playwright other than keep him in mind.

Nonetheless, the young playwright moved to Hollywood, settled into inexpensive digs, and began to write screenplays. "They were terrible at first," Kazan claims. But he kept at it, and his work gradually gained recognition. His first sale was to a would-be producer who needed somebody who would work cheap. His second was to a producer who made so many changes that Kazan took his name off the credits.

A fierce determination to win on his own terms helps mark Nick Kazan as an outstanding writer. Largely self-taught, he started from ground zero and, on his own, wrote and rewrote script after script, developing his talent until he rose into the upper echelon of his profession and took his place among our most successful screenwriters. He has also become a behind-the-scenes mover and shaker in the screenwriters' struggle for recognition of their primary contributions to motion pictures.

Nick Kazan is one of the most delightful people I have ever met. It is a pleasure to know him and to introduce him to you.

FROUG: I think one of the most impressive screenplays I have ever
          seen is *Reversal of Fortune*. How did you get involved in that
          project?

KAZAN: I had just finished *Patty Hearst* when I was offered *Reversal*.
          I was kind of depressed because I put a lot of work into the
          Hearst script and I liked it very much. The film had been made,
          but it was made in a very different way. My script was very
          raucous. But it was made as a very existential film about the loss
          of identity. It was a good film, but it was not what I intended.
          Patty Hearst herself said, when she saw the final film, that she
          had been afraid that it would be sex, drugs, and rock and roll, and
          she was very relieved that it wasn't. Well, my script was sex, drugs
          and rock and roll. It was a black comedy. I thought it was the
          perfect way to do the material because what happened—the real
          event—was so outlandish. The only thing you could do was
          laugh at it.

          My response to material is often unconscious. I try not to
          take jobs just to be employed, and I try not to do a screenplay
          just because I love what the story says. Because, ultimately, if I do
          that, my enthusiasm flags. I have to have an unconscious response

to the material, and I don't know what my response to the Dershowitz material was. As best I can remember it, I took the *Reversal* job just to get my mind off *Patty Hearst*, to combat depression, to be working again—the worst of reasons.

On the other hand, as soon as I read the source material, Alan Dershowitz's book, I started writing dialogue and I actually wrote, among other things, the final sequence of the movie: the scene where Claus walks into the drugstore and asks for insulin and we see the expression on the clerk's face, and then Claus says, "I'm just kidding." It came to me immediately. I wrote that scene right off the bat, and that was part of how I knew I had to do it; the material claimed me. When I start writing dialogue, I know that the story is fertile for me.

FROUG: Is this before you write an outline?

KAZAN: Before anything. They just sent me the book. I didn't have the job, but I just started writing. Sometimes when this happens, I don't know who is talking. I am just writing something that floats out from the basic material. So I took the job based on whatever this unconscious response was. Once I took the job and started to really look at it, I became very, very concerned.

FROUG: You had the court transcript of an appeal?

KAZAN: I had six thousand pages of transcript. It took me about two months just to read and annotate the transcript so I knew where to find things. Of course, everyone else who read it looked at it from a legal perspective. I was looking at it from a dramatic perspective, and I found things in there that a dramatist would find that the legal minds would not find. In some ways, the film was partly a detective story. It was very exciting because

I'd read it one day and come home and say, "I think he's innocent." Then I'd read it the next day and come home and say, "I
think he is guilty." I kept going back and forth.

FROUG: You had to deal with the famous Harvard professor and
ACLU expert Alan Dershowitz, a real person you are putting
into a drama. How did you deal with him? Was he difficult?

KAZAN: First I read his appeal, which was beautifully written. Very,
very simple. It is written in layman's language, and it's very
powerful and persuasive. Then I went to Boston to see Alan. I
grew up in New York, and all my friends were Jewish, so I figured
I would understand him right away. I didn't. He was a much more
contradictory character than the mensches I grew up with.

FROUG: Did he tell you how to write the screenplay?

KAZAN: He didn't try to do that at all. In fact, in person he is a lot
like Woody Allen. He tells one funny story after another. You ask
him a question and he tells you a funny story. He has a kind of
schlubby aspect. He can obviously get his dander up and so forth.
One of the problems in writing the screenplay was that I couldn't
portray this Woody Allen aspect because everyone would just say,
"Oh, they're doing Alan Dershowitz as Woody Allen? Why?" I
would actually be portraying Alan Dershowitz, but no one would
believe it. So I had to develop a dramatic character. Dershowitz
had some kind of vague script approval—approval of the way he
looked as a lawyer. It was enough to bother me because you never
want a real live person to have script approval. His son, Elon, who
turned out to be an enormous asset, was a co-producer on the
movie, and I was concerned about having the son looking over my
shoulder. My biggest problem portraying Dershowitz was how do

I make a complete human being, a protagonist? He was already fighting for truth and justice and the American way but he was also defending the devil here; he had to have some rough edges or no one would empathize with him—he'd just be a cardboard cutout of a good guy.

FROUG: He would have been boring, but he wasn't boring in the movie.

KAZAN: I hope not. I kept looking for a flaw, and of course, if I brought up something that was not true of him, it would be very offensive to him because it wasn't true. If I brought up something that was true, he would be even more offended because no one wants their real flaws in a movie. So finally I came up with what I thought was an elegant solution, because it was a flaw but it fit with the story: In pursuit of justice, he started to get snappy and angry with his colleagues.

FROUG: A working fanatic.

KAZAN: Yes. He would become a fanatic, a slave driver. Thematically, it fit. So I went to propose this to him at a fancy restaurant in New York. As we sat down and before I could open my mouth—the guy must be psychic—Dershowitz says, "There is one thing I want you to know about me: I never lose my temper. I don't care how little sleep I have. I don't care how close we are to a deadline or how badly things are going. I always keep an even keel. I never get mad at my students or collaborators." I burst out laughing because he had just taken my hand away from me. I explained what I was about to do and that I needed to have something, otherwise no one would like him as a character. He reluctantly agreed to let me portray him in this fashion.

FROUG: How did you go about structuring this screenplay? It is a very unusual structure. It's told as a flashback, then it flashes forward and back again. Time becomes irrelevant. All the while, you are dealing with the story being told by the victim who is alive but in a coma. It's one of the most unusual structures I have ever seen. How did you approach that dramatically?

KAZAN: Well, as for having the woman in a coma telling the story, this came from a chance remark by Ed Pressman, the producer of the film, who suggested with a giggle that I tell it from Sunny's point of view.

At the outset, I realized I was going to have to summarize two trials which had already occurred and a mountain of evidence. It seemed like a ridiculous way to begin a movie. Well, the obvious way to do it was to have Dershowitz summarize everything, but that's so boring. So I remembered Ed Pressman's giggle and I thought, "Why not?" Immediately I wrote the beginning narration and the final narration. It just came right out of me, so I knew that was a good idea.

FROUG: Your instinct told you.

KAZAN: My instinct told me, and it immediately solved the problem. I could summarize everything, but it would have this odd cast and this peculiar sense of humor that I felt was necessary to tell the story anyway. Once I found that, then I looked at the whole story. I saw that the appeal was essentially based on about three, four, five, or six primary points of attack. I realized I couldn't make any one of them carry the whole weight of the movie; none of them was strong enough. I had to use all of them. So I imagined that I was a juggler. I thought, if I throw one ball up in the air and then throw a couple more up, when the first one comes down and we gain some new information, we have progress. Then I throw that one back up and add a new one. We won't know ever exactly where we are in the movie because one of the stories will be nearing its conclusion just as another is beginning. The audience and the lawyers were trying to keep track of all these different strands, hoping one or two or three of them would become really juicy and supply grounds for reversal of the conviction.

FROUG: Are you analyzing this as you go, or did you lay this out before you started?

KAZAN: The way I work is that I write notes. I don't use cards. I just write notes to myself. A lot of it is dialogue. I do many outlines. In the first couple of weeks, I'll attempt an outline. Usually I don't get very far, maybe twenty pages in, and I don't know what comes next, so I stop. Then a couple of weeks later I'll try the outline again. Eventually I have a fairly detailed outline. However, I almost always depart from it as I write because the rhythm of the organic being is different from the rhythm that you anticipate before you create the piece.

FROUG: So you don't worry about wandering off a bit while you're writing?

KAZAN: Well, in my experience, it hurts if you truly wander— you'll suffer for it later and realize you shouldn't have wandered; you should have stayed on the path. But if you mosey a little bit off the path, that's good. What often happens is that you find out that a scene you thought you needed is extrane- ous. Or you will find that you have two scenes that are both

"Eventually I have a fairly detailed outline. However, I almost always depart from it as I write because the rhythm of the organic being is different from the rhythm that you anticipate before you create the piece."

[288]

powerful and you need a rest in between. It's almost like orchestrating a piece of music.

FROUG: In the case of *Reversal*, you always have a single line, a driving line or action line: Is he guilty or isn't he guilty? Yet, because of the way you wrote the screenplay, in the end we really don't know for sure.

KAZAN: I wanted to call the film *The Devil's Advocate*. In my mind, the thematic construct was, we're trying to get justice for the devil. Even though there was something clearly malevolent about Claus, he still might be innocent. He was guilty of something, but probably not guilty of injecting his wife with insulin—which is what he was accused of. In our system of justice, you can't convict someone of murder without saying that he did it here on this day, in this manner, for this reason. In that sense, he was, I believe, legally "innocent." It's quite possible that he didn't kill her, but that he contributed to her death or her deepening coma.

FROUG: Through negligence?

KAZAN: Through negligence or something. Perhaps he allowed her to take drugs and did nothing to save her. There are many possible causes for the aura of guilt that surrounds him. Some of those causes verge on the illegal. Other causes are more benign. So even though he seems like the devil, he still deserves a fair trial. That was the driving thematic line.

FROUG: You did a magnificent job. Let's talk about *At Close Range*, another of your excellent screenplays. There is a ring of truth about it. Is it based on a true story?

KAZAN: It is based on a true story. There was supposed to be a card that said so, but there wasn't. I always regret that because the story I was trying to tell was a Greek tragedy, and it was very important to me that these things really happened: a father who kills his children. The kind of thing you just wouldn't believe had it not happened.

FROUG: Do you think that the director had a different view than you did?

KAZAN: The director had a somewhat different view. To be honest, Bill, I have gone on record in the past criticizing various people who made the film, and I don't want to do that anymore. I will say that due to a variety of circumstances, the raw power of the basic material I was given was somewhat diminished in the filmmaking. For one thing, we didn't have enough money.

FROUG: The movie had moments of greatness. It still had a lot of power.

KAZAN: It's funny, it's the script that really transformed my career: first when I wrote, because it was so widely admired, then again when it was made. It was my first solo credit. When you have a film about difficult material that gets made, then you are not a virgin anymore. People think, "Oh, this guy can carry a serious film." Everybody wanted to hire me.

FROUG: Let me ask about one where you can't blame the director, *Dream Lover*, because you were both the screenwriter and the director. When I was at my local video store, they told me, "We don't have the unrated version of *Dream Lover*; we only have the R-rated version." What's the difference?

KAZAN: Well, when the film was going to come out in video, the company called me and said that more money could be made, mostly by them, if we had more "sexy footage."

FROUG: You had shot more intimate love scenes?

KAZAN: I didn't add that much. The unrated version wasn't that different, but if you say "four minutes of never-before-seen material," everyone thinks they are seeing something which is a lot sexier, and that's the one they want. I put back a scene at the very end of the movie which is thirty seconds long and had no erotic content whatsoever.

FROUG: Are you satisfied with the movie?

KAZAN: I like the film. I think I did a good job. There were things which a more experienced director might have done better, but I am proud of the film. It's an odd film.

FROUG: Do you plan to continue directing?

KAZAN: I am not sure. There are some things I'd like to direct. There were aspects of the process that were very unpleasant. It wasn't all fun. It took a very long time. We had reshoots. I'll tell you a funny, horrible story: The film didn't test as well as they would have liked. So the studio decided that they wanted to put a slasher scene at the end of the movie. Whatever the film's limitations may be, it ended in a very clever and dramatically satisfying way. I resisted their efforts. In fact, I refused to do it, at which point I was told that I would be sued.

FROUG: What did they mean by a slasher ending?

KAZAN: They wanted the lead, the villain actually, but she was kind of a hero in my eyes, to suddenly run amok and start killing people with a knife.

FROUG: That's out of nowhere.

KAZAN: Totally out of nowhere and quite absurd because, at the end of the film, she believes she has won. It was totally out of character, so I tried to resist it. But I was told I had to do it by my contract, and if I didn't, it would cost me half a million dollars—more money than I made on the film. So I decided quite reluctantly to shoot it. I had some minor changes that I wanted in my ending, so I agreed to shoot theirs if I could shoot mine first. Well, we shot two days of my ending. In the interim, between the time the film was shot and the time of the reshoot, Mädchen Amick, the actress who played Lena, got pregnant. So we shot my reshoot and one day of their ending, and then she had pregnancy complications and couldn't continue. We had to stop. They thought she and I orchestrated this and that she was faking it.

FROUG: Did you have something to do with the pregnancy?

KAZAN: I had nothing to do with the pregnancy and nothing to do with her physical problems. But they had to get many doctors' opinions before they would believe us. Thank god it happened. If their slasher ending had been used, the film would have been a terrible embarrassment. I would have taken my name off it. So if you read the tail credits on this movie, you will see that the first special thank-you goes to the actress's daughter, who at the time we made the credits wasn't even born. All we knew was that it was going to be a girl. The first thank-you was to an unborn child who had saved us.

FROUG: *Frances* is a fascinating film with your name on the screenplay. Please tell me about it.

KAZAN: I was hired to rewrite *Frances*. I was very fortunate because the previous writers, the team of Eric Bergren and Chris

DeVore, who'd also written *The Elephant Man*, had done wonderful work. But they'd written ten or twelve drafts, most of them distinct from the others. Two drafts were over 200 pages. In one of them, Frances Farmer wasn't even the protagonist. It was astonishing to me that every single draft was beautifully written; but by the point I came on, Eric and Chris were burned out. They had to be. I believe it was really a case where the producers had abused the goodwill and talent of the writers, having them try every imaginable approach to the material.

I was able to keep most of what Chris and Eric had done, and I hope improve it in a few key areas. Much of what I did was see what was there and enrich it. I believe that a good script usually has a myth at its center, and once you find the myth, you know how to focus your story. The myth at the center of *Frances* was clear to me: Frances Farmer was a woman who told the truth at all costs and was punished for it. That's simple, powerful, universal. It could easily have been the basis of a Greek myth. It's also emotionally compelling. We all respond to truth and admire characters that tell the truth. And many of us have been punished in one way or another for telling the truth.

FROUG: That theory of a myth at the center of a story is fascinating.

KAZAN: It's not always easy to find that core. Sometimes the myth is elusive. But when you find it, it's an enormous help. And if you can't find it, if you have no idea what the myth is, you're usually in trouble.

FROUG: Maybe the movie resonates because you found the myth.

KAZAN: I don't know, of course, whether Bergren and DeVore had a similar idea of what the movie was about. Often I find that I

"Sometimes the myth is elusive. But when you find it, it's an enormous help. And if you can't find it, if you have no idea what the myth is, you're usually in trouble."

discover the myth after I've written the first draft: The unconscious intention declares itself.

FROUG: Should a writer always know what a story is about—the
underlying meaning, the theme?

KAZAN: Absolutely. But it's best, I think, to write out of unconscious compulsion. I never choose what to write. I let the stories
choose me. In that way I only write what I am absolutely
compelled to write. If I am not forced to write it, obligated by
my own imagination, then I don't do it. I find something else.

FROUG:;   You have a new movie coming out soon. Please tell me
about it.

KAZAN: It's *Bicentennial Man*, with Robin Williams; Chris Colum-
bus is directing. It's about a robot who seems to have something
resembling a human conscience. In the end, it's about this robot's
quest to be recognized as a human.

FROUG: Is this an original screenplay?

KAZAN: It is an adaptation of a short story by Isaac Asimov.

FROUG: How long did you spend on the screenplay?

KAZAN: I spent about four months doing the first draft. When I
received the short story, I immediately sat down and wrote ten
pages of dialogue.

FROUG: So you knew this project was for you?

KAZAN: Yes. But when I finished the first draft, they told me that it
wasn't going to work. Essentially, the movie is a love story. The
robot comes into a family where there is a three-year-old. He
bonds with the three-year-old. They are really good friends for
this woman's entire life. And at the end of her life, she introduces

him to her granddaughter, who looks just like her and is played by the same actress. This granddaughter and the robot essentially fall in love. So it's about his quest to be recognized at a political level, and also at an emotional level.

FROUG: Have you seen the movie?

KAZAN: I have seen the movie, yes.

FROUG: Do you like it?

KAZAN: Well, Bill, the process, as so often happens, was painful. The director spoke to me twice. He was extremely cordial but wanted nothing to do with me. He did a lot of rewrites. When I first saw the preview, I was pleased that my structure was there, that the character I'd created still existed in some form, and that many of the scenes I loved most were still in the movie. The second time I saw it, I was appalled at the changes and how profound they seemed to be. As they say, God, or any visage of same, is in the details, which work well in a really good movie and are somehow off, really off, in a film that's flawed. Add up a dozen things that are deftly done and you have quality. If a dozen things go wrong, the audience won't forgive you. Sometimes the differences are quite subtle, sometimes not. I probably won't know for sure how I feel about this thing for another ten years. Screenwriting is the only business where you're glad if people like the movie because of whatever remnants of your work remain, and equally happy if they hate it because of what was badly rewritten. But there is one story about this film that I think is worth telling because it may give some kind of comfort to other writers. It's about a problem that's going on in Hollywood right now. Producers are taking advantage of writers. Many of the writers are doing what is called a "producer's polish."

FROUG: A free rewrite?

KAZAN: A free rewrite, exactly. This is a movie where I did a free rewrite at my own insistence and against the wishes of the studio. I turned in the first draft and they told me that it was never going to work having this grandmother and granddaughter; the robot should have a relationship with only one person. I said, "No, this is essential to the robot's problem. The robot is a machine. You know he is a machine because he outlives all his human friends." They said, "No, we want you to redo it with just one woman, even if it's only a hundred years." I went away very depressed. After two weeks, I said, "Let me just try one more time my way. If it doesn't work, then we will do it your way." They said, "We don't want you to do that. How long is it going to take?" I said, "a couple of weeks." Well, it took me three months. I spent three months of my own time, and on my own dime. I turned it in to them, and everybody—the producer and the junior studio executives—said it didn't work. So they asked if they should give it to David Vogel, head of production at Disney at that point. I said, "Don't bother. Everybody agreed that it doesn't work. Don't show it." As soon as Vogel heard that he wasn't going to see it, he wanted to see it. He read it and decided it did work, and—in my view—the movie was saved. So here was a case where I followed my passion. I ignored what they said. I did it on my own time, spent three months without being paid for rewriting the script, and was rewarded for doing so.

FROUG: It's a happy ending, which is rare.

KAZAN: It is rare, exactly.

FROUG: Which leads me to my next question. Tell me about the origins of the Thursday Night group.

KAZAN: Frank Pierson and Callie Khouri and Phil Robinson were together at some function, and they said, "You know, screenwriters like each other; we get along well. But in our rooms, we are isolated. We don't see each other. It wouldn't work for directors; they would all be jealous of each other. It wouldn't work for actors. But it would work for us. We could just get together casually and talk about our lives." So they invited twenty or thirty people they knew to have dinner and talk. And we did.

FROUG: Where did you meet?

KAZAN: At our houses. I forget which one. Then we said, let's do it again. So we started doing it every month for a while. The first twenty or thirty invited other people that they knew, and the word spread. It became a very social atmosphere. But also a political atmosphere, which was very good for us because we shared our problems.

FROUG: Which led to the negotiation with Columbia Pictures, where, at long last, screenwriters under certain circumstances can get a percentage of the gross?

KAZAN: At the Thursday Night group there were two kinds of primary concerns. One was creative rights and the other was a lack of respect. At one of these meetings Robert Towne said, "What we should be doing is getting gross. If we get gross, then respect will follow. And if we get respect, then our creative rights will be recognized." So a few of us made very subtle inquiries around town, and Sony responded. So we cut off all other conversations and negotiated in secret with them for six months. John Calley was there at the beginning. Some of the meetings were with Lucy Fischer, but primarily with Amy Pascal. The most important aspect of the whole deal was that we got gross for a lot of screenwriters. The most amazing part of this deal, which is often obscured, is that thirty writers made a commitment to Sony, but in return, I believe, probably 500 writers are technically eligible to get gross at that studio.

FROUG: By selling a screenplay for a million bucks?

KAZAN: Even if they never sold a screenplay for a million bucks. If their price, their hard price without the bonus, is seven hundred fifty thousand dollars or, and this is the category which includes a lot of people, if they have ever been nominated for an Academy Award or a Writers Guild Award, they are eligible.

FROUG: That's a big plus.

KAZAN: One studio executive said to me, "Directors never would have done this for each other. Actors never would have done this for each other. But writers would."

FROUG: When you realize that only about eight or ten top-of-the-line MGM screenwriters founded the Screenwriters Guild, which became the Writers Guild of America, you understand the kind of solidarity writers have. I think it's just terrific, and I congratulate you because I know you are one of the movers and shakers who made it happen.

KAZAN: Thank you. While we're at it, Bill, there's something I need to say. When I first moved to Santa Monica in 1976, I knew very little about screenwriting. I'd written plays and tried to write screenplays, and none of them were any good. A friend gave me a tattered copy of a book to read. The book was literally held together by rubber bands; it had been passed around to so many writers that you had to read it like an unbound copy of a novel, picking up individual pages and turning them over. That book was *The Screenwriter Looks at the Screenwriter*, your first collection of interviews. It contained more practical knowledge than any other book I've seen, except, perhaps, your subsequent volumes. So I want to say thanks for that book. Because of my experience with it, I am particularly thrilled to be included in this one.

FROUG: Thanks for your generous words. My books aside, what is your advice for aspiring screenwriters?

KAZAN: Keep writing and, somehow or other, your second screenplay gets better than your first, and your fifth one is a lot better than your first. You just get better by doing it. It's the same as learning to be a carpenter. The first bench you build is not as good as the hundredth. You learn by doing. If you teach yourself, you develop your own sense of doing it and your own style and process and your work becomes idiosyncratic. It has a mark that's distinct from anyone else.

FROUG: It's like your fingerprint.

KAZAN: It's like your fingerprint. When people pick up your work, they can tell it's you. More importantly, at the beginning, they don't know you, but they can tell it's different—it catches their attention. Whereas, if you learn to write by following a certain paradigm, you do everything the way everyone else does; your screenplay looks like everyone else's. It just blends into an endless stream of similar pieces of work.

"The first bench you build is not as good as the hundredth. You learn by doing."

•

FILMOGRAPHY

Writer

1982   *Frances* (shared credit)

1983   *At Close Range*

1984   *Patty Hearst*, based on a book by Patty Hearst and Alvin Moscow

1985   *Reversal of Fortune*, based on the book by Alan M. Dershowitz

1986   *Mobsters* (shared credit)

1987   *Dream Lover*

1988   *Matilda* (shared, with Robin Swicord), based on the novel by Roald Dahl

1989   *Fallen*

1990   *Homegrown* (shared credit)

1991   *Bicentennial Man*, based on a short story by Isaac Asimov and a novel by Isaac Asimov and Robert Silberberg

Producer

1990   *Reversal of Fortune*, co-producer

1991   *Matilda*, co-producer

1992   *Fallen*, executive producer

Director

1986   *The Edge*, television movie

1994   *Dream Lover*

The Screenwriter's Screenwriter

An Interview with

Eric Roth

"I think you only do what sort of thrills you, and you have to hope you reflect what other people will respond to."

—Eric Roth

Those of you who read my first *Zen and the Art of Screenwriting* probably remember Eric Roth, the Oscar-winning screenwriter of *Forrest Gump*. Roth began his screenwriting career early, turning out award-winning screenplays almost before he could talk and winning the prestigious Samuel Goldwyn Award at UCLA, where he took a directed studies course from me. I had nothing to teach Eric Roth, but I learned a lot.

Now, almost three decades later, the kid from Tinseltown is grown up, a grandfather who not only wins at the track (playing the horses is his hobby) but has gone the distance to be the Citation as well as Secretariat of screenwriters. Nobody comes close to this writer's track record.

It is always a very special treat for me to chat with Eric Roth. He is a gentleman, a friend, a straight shooter, and an all-around wonderful human being.

FROUG: What leads you to take on a project? You know you are going to invest a year or more of your time writing the screenplay. What is it that grabs you and says, "This one I'm going to do"?

ROTH: Oddly enough, I am fairly easy about that. Maybe I'm not as selective as I should be. I go backward: I know what I can't do. There are some high-concept pieces like a seven-year-old kid who goes to Harvard that would not work for me.

FROUG: Too much of a gimmick?

ROTH: Well, I'm not talking about some problem child. I liked
Little Man Tate. I thought it was a good movie. It's just that I try
to avoid one-hook stories that don't seem to have any kind of
scope. But I am interested in almost anything.

FROUG: I know you were reluctant to take on *The Insider* and that
you ended up collaborating, which you rarely do.

ROTH: Yeah. I had said no to Michael Mann a number of times
for a number of reasons. One, I wasn't really sure that we could
make it bigger than a shoebox. In other words, I didn't want to
do it for television, a TV movie. I wanted to break out of that
and make it have more scope, not that TV movies can't have
scope, but they don't often have the opportunity to develop it.

FROUG: What did you see that elevated the tobacco industry
whistleblower's story beyond a TV movie?

ROTH: I also was hesitant to do it because I was sort of questioning whether I had the ability to write, in a creative way, the kind
of business talk you need. But Michael kept feeding me stuff
about the characters, and I got the chance to meet Lowell
Bergman and other people involved in the actual story. I started
evaluating and investigating it. I felt some sensitivity toward the
characters. Once I got hooked into the characters, it becomes a
very interesting story and a great challenge. In simple terms, it's
sort of a very unlikely buddy picture, since these people would
probably not be seen in the same room together. And they were
also both flawed men. And there were these wonderful, huge
themes about ethics and freedom of speech—tremendous
issues—so that, in the long run, it was worth doing.

FROUG: The results are terrific. But you say that this story was a great challenge?

ROTH: Absolutely. It was a huge challenge. But I don't take jobs because they are easy. They are all challenges. You have to find stories that you are passionate about. It becomes a great adventure.

FROUG: Were you challenged very much on *The Horse Whisperer*?

ROTH: Well, I think I was, except that Bob Redford and I weren't seeing the same movie. I think I finally lost my creative spark for it, but it was a challenge to try to constrain the melodrama and make it what I hoped would be a more interesting movie. I thought it was challenging also because it was a modern Western and the theme was based on interesting material, which sort of evolved. But, eventually, I wasn't given the support I needed. Bob and I had different thoughts about the film. We were seeing different movies.

FROUG: So basically you had two different endings?

ROTH: The truth was that we had a number of different endings. We had an ending when he died, which was similar in kind though not in performance to what happened in the book. There was another scene where he slept with the woman. I wrote them all for Bob. He had an A and B choice for everything. So when we parted company he could choose from any of them, and we could discuss what was right and what was wrong about them.

FROUG: How much pain do you feel when you've written a script that you love and it is rewritten by somebody else?

ROTH: I guess it always hurts a little bit. Personally, it's a sense of rejection. I don't think anybody wants rejection. You'd like to be patted on the head and told "great job." It bothers you, but you have to learn to use it in certain situations. I have a problem when the people who rewrite want to take credit for something they didn't write, and don't want to share credit for the hard work you've done.

FROUG: It seems to me that there's an ongoing rewriting problem among screenwriters.

ROTH: There is sort of a revolving rewrite situation going on.

FROUG: Every writer who rewrites some other writer wants to call it his or her own movie?

ROTH: I guess, when they take over, they begin to feel emotionally and psychologically that everything that works is theirs. But when you come to the pure light of day, the fair thing generally is a shared credit.

FROUG: That's what you did with Michael Mann on *The Insider*, although I suspect that you had to do most of the actual writing.

ROTH: I think I did the original heavy lifting, but Michael did a lot of work, and he deserves the shared writing credit.

FROUG: Who is your favorite screenwriter?

ROTH: I don't know if there is one. Robert Bolt was a great screenwriter. He had the opportunity to work with a great director, David Lean. I think Bo Goldman is a great writer on various subjects. Alvin Sargent is a wonderful writer. Waldo Salt and Dalton Trumbo were wonderful writers. Screenwriting is an oddball field. We are not novelists, not poets, but a combination of many, many things.

FROUG: Why can't screenwriters get respect?

ROTH: I guess because we have no copyright rights. The play-wrights have it, but we take assignments, we take jobs. The spec scripts and original work are not on assignment, but screen-writers are at the tail end of the system that treats writers as if we were interchangeable. To some extent there is some truth to that: There's a point at which we rewrite each other. Still, I think the writer is slowly getting more respect.

FROUG: Do you think that the "film by" credit will be defeated finally?

ROTH: No, I actually don't. I think it's a hard issue. I am not questioning the value of the word, but the movie ends up being particularly the director's vision when all is said and done. He is the one who casts the movie. He is the one who moves the art director around to the way he wants the film to look. He chooses the film stock, the colors, and works with the cinema-tographer to give the film a feel. He finds the music, the sound effects, and everything else. And at the end of the day, I think the film has more of a relationship with the director than it has with the writer.

FROUG: Why do world audiences seem to prefer American movies to their own homegrown movies?

ROTH: That's a great question. I never thought about that. I was going to say that they may like things foreign to them, but I don't think that's true—there are a lot of American movies they don't like because they have no relationship to the subject matter. I guess there is something sort of magical about Hollywood product. In a way it's guileless. I mean, Hollywood will do either brave or stupid things with a sort of magical quality. I don't

"I guess there is something sort of magical about Hollywood product. In a way it's guileless. I mean, Hollywood will do either brave or stupid things with a sort of magical quality."

know how to define what that is. I am sure the same is true about European films or worldwide films, but maybe not with the same regularity. What do you think?

FROUG: Well, I think it has to do with the pace and energy that goes into American movies.

ROTH: I am sure that filmmakers in France or Holland or anywhere have energy equal to ours.

FROUG: The *New York Times* had a recent article reporting that the French film critics are battling the French directors because the directors say that the critics are killing French films. French audiences are lining up for American films but not French films. And the French critics respond, "It's true. But on the whole, American movies are better than French movies."

ROTH: I wonder if "better" is the right word. I wonder if it's that our films are more unique in some ways. I can't imagine *Forrest Gump* being anything but an American movie. Certain movies are traditionally American. What makes a movie American, I don't know.

FROUG: Did *Forrest Gump* do well worldwide?

ROTH: Very well. It did better foreign than it did domestic.

FROUG: Doesn't that kind of dispute what you just said?

ROTH: No. It says that it's a unique piece of Americana. I don't know what becomes a universal language, but if you could bottle it, you could make a billion dollars. *Titanic* did phenomenally well all around the world.

FROUG: It did. And a French film critic said he liked *There's Something About Mary* better than most French movies. Go figure.

ROTH: The movie did such tremendous business that I assume people were enjoying it when they went to see it, and they must have thought it was funny. Humor is often international.

FROUG: You started your career writing spec screenplays, right?

ROTH: The first one I wrote was spec.

FROUG: *Harmonica Patriots*?

ROTH: Yeah. I am sorry about that title. It won the Samuel Goldwyn Screenwriting Award at UCLA back in '80. I also simultaneously wrote *Fifty/Fifty*.

FROUG: Which was the best student screenplay I've ever read in my life. Then Fox bought it and gutted it and changed the title to *Nickel Ride*, which had nothing whatsoever to do with the movie.

ROTH: True. But what are you going to do?

FROUG: And you then went under contract to Universal?

ROTH: Eventually, yes.

FROUG: You wrote some of the *Airplane* movies.

ROTH: That was at Universal. Bad work.

FROUG: When did you move on to good work? And what made the difference?

ROTH: I don't know. The truth is, I would always take jobs that were bad jobs just to keep working. But I think I was always a pretty good writer, and my writing has grown. I think I always had a capability of creating depth of characterization. The weakest part of my work is storytelling. You do work you can do. I guess I am just like anybody else. I am still a working writer; I just have more opportunity than some other writers.

FROUG: Eric, to put it nicely, that's bullshit. You are the greatest writer I ever encountered in my sixteen years of teaching at UCLA and a couple more years of teaching at other film schools. You're in a class by yourself.

ROTH: Bless your heart. The truth is, I have also written *Airport*. I've started some lectures by saying that I am the guy who wrote *Airport '79,* and now I will probably say *The Insider* and *Forrest Gump*. So I am just saying that you learn and grow, and that there is a breadth of work you do. Some things you do because you need to do them, and some things you do out of love. Fortunately, if you get successful, you get to do a lot more things out of love.

FROUG: Now you can pick and choose?

ROTH: Yeah.

FROUG: Do you still write spec scripts or do you have too many assignments?

ROTH: I haven't really written anything on spec in a long time. I just go on from job to job.

FROUG: Do you work seven days a week?

ROTH: Not unless I am under the gun. Usually I work five-day weeks. I start work about nine o'clock in the morning. I find I can be creative for about four hours, and then I go screw around—go to the races or go to play with my kids. I will start writing again at nine or ten at night and I write couple of hours, maybe three hours, until I'm tired. I sleep about four hours. And then I get up at four-thirty or five o'clock or earlier and write for maybe an hour. Then I go back to sleep for half an hour.

FROUG: How much do you rewrite yourself?

ROTH: I rewrite every day. I start with page one. Someone once told me something mathematically interesting about this process. If I always start with page one, I have to spend a lot more time on page one than I would on page one through twenty-five. It's sort of funny, I never thought of it that way.

FROUG: I always held to the theory, which you are proving wrong, that once you start you have to go through to Fade Out before you come back and rewrite.

ROTH: I've done that too. But basically I go back every day to page one. That takes me a number of months until I feel I don't have to look at the first forty pages or so anymore. Even today, before we began talking, I started working on page thirty-something of a screenplay I've been working on for a very long time.

FROUG: How long have you been on this script?

ROTH: About nine months.

FROUG: Which script is it?

ROTH: This one is for Robin Williams. It's about a man with twenty-four multiple personalities.

FROUG: The whole question of multiple personalities is debatable, right?

ROTH: Yeah. There are questions whether it actually exists.

FROUG: Are you taking a position on it?

ROTH: Nope. I am being slightly ambiguous. I take a position that the man is emotionally disturbed in some form. At the end, you have to judge for yourself. But I think he will make an interesting sort of ride. It's a fascinating thing.

FROUG: Very. How much research did you do?

ROTH: I am not a big researcher, to be honest with you. But this one has a book attached to it that the gentleman who has the condition wrote.

FROUG: It's an adaptation?

ROTH: It is an adaptation of a kind, yeah. I did some research. I have someone whom I can talk to about this multiple personality problem, which is called dissociative disorder. But you've got to tell the story first. The technical people come in and provide the medical accuracy as I need it.

FROUG: You are not disturbed that there have been a couple of award-winning movies about multiple personalities, *Sybil* being one of them?

ROTH: Not really, because I think I am taking a different tack with it. First of all, I don't think too many have been done about a male. I also have the arrogance to think I am going to do it differently than anybody else. I think it is very different than what anybody else would have done. I am so proud of it. I'm sort of anxious to get the film made.

FROUG: We are always telling new writers to come up with something original, and most writers would be scared off from a subject that has been covered by several movies and books. Yet you plowed right in; it doesn't concern you.

ROTH: No, it doesn't concern me that it has been done before, because I think I have another take on it and am doing it in some fresh way. I would be concerned if there was another movie being done right now on the same subject, even though I probably would have the arrogance to think that I could do it better.

FROUG: You never know when you are writing whether somebody else is writing the same thing, true?

ROTH: You have no way of knowing. So you take a different path. Everybody is different.

FROUG: Is there much real communication between screenwriters?

ROTH: Almost none. At least I don't have much communication with others, except maybe a dozen people. I have become kind of friendly with a few since the group called the Thursday Night group started meeting somewhat irregularly on a regular basis. But the group hasn't met in a while. Screenwriting is a lonely, kind of isolated profession basically. Unless you are a TV writer or you happen to work with a collaborator, you are alone most of the time. That's just what it is. I like that, but some people may not.

FROUG: What do you think is the difference between a TV movie and a theatrical movie?

ROTH: Billy Crystal said, "One is bigger than life and the other is smaller than life." In a movie theater, first of all, you have a captive audience. It may not be happily captive, but it is captive for a while, so you are able to explore some different things. The size of the screen really has something to do with it. You get a bigger emotional scale in a movie. Because theatrical movies have much bigger budgets, you can bring in textures and colors and sights and sounds that you may not get in a TV movie. But I think they are both about the quality of the writing. Look at the *Playhouse 90*s and some of the early television dramas and some of the work that is being done now, like *The Sopranos*—the writing is so great that the shows are certainly equal to any movie.

FROUG: Would you advise a new screenwriter to write a TV movie or a theatrical movie?

ROTH: A writer should go whatever way feels like the best way to go with the story. But I don't think you can be as visually creative in TV as you can with a motion picture. Also, don't forget that, in a movie, you are sitting with strangers in a crowded room. It's pretty nice. You get a whole different range of emotional reactions than sitting alone at home watching TV.

FROUG: But if you are writing a TV movie, you can deal with subjects like AIDS or abortion—controversial subject matter that the big screen won't deal with.

ROTH: Absolutely. I think one of the real advantages to writing television, even episodic television, is that you have a chance to do maybe five or six phenomenal shows a year. You can't do that in movies.

FROUG: Is that because the studios are afraid they will alienate some segment of the population?

ROTH: Maybe. Yeah. *The Insider* is a perfect example. Why haven't we had great box-office success? Maybe it's too serious. It is a risk to do that kind of movie, as well made as I think it is. But in TV you can do it more easily, and it will not be as risky financially.

FROUG: What is your take on movie audiences today? Do you believe that most Hollywood films are basically aimed at teenagers, and they don't want serious subjects?

ROTH: I'm one who disagrees with that. I give audiences more credit than others do. I think it depends on what the issue is.

FROUG: Maybe some of the excitement of our work is that we never know what an audience is going to buy or not buy.

ROTH: Absolutely so. I think you only do what sort of thrills you, and you have to hope you reflect what other people will respond to.

FROUG: You don't try to second-guess what the audience will buy when you are writing?

ROTH: No. The only thing I will try to second-guess is what project offered to me is going to get made of the some four or five different things that have been offered and that I have an equal passion for in some way. Which one will have the best chance of getting done? After a year, you hope that it bears some fruit. Otherwise your screenplay sits on the shelf.

FROUG: Do you have many that don't get made?

ROTH: A few. I have been fortunate. I think my ratio is probably about two to one.

FROUG: What about the CIA movie we discussed the last time we talked?

ROTH: We are still talking about it. It keeps going somehow. I now have Robert De Niro to direct if we are able to get some seed money. And I have been doing some changes Bob wanted. They are not particularly significant.

FROUG: Once you have a screenplay, it really is a property? It's never dead?

ROTH: I don't think it is ever dead. This one is kind of a universal idea. Some ideas may eventually get dated. But I don't think this one is dated. I think the themes are things that we are always interested in. It's a dark piece. On face value it may not be commercial, so it's tough to get done. But it's worth doing.

FROUG: It's a history of the CIA, right?

ROTH: Well, it's my own version of that. It's fiction. It's the first twenty-five years of the CIA. It follows one young man as he approaches Yale and goes into a secret society, which was there, and then becomes one of the group that eventually founded the CIA.

FROUG: In terms of all these projects, do you tend to keep working one on top of the other?

ROTH: Actually, I do. I really only like to write one at a time, but I don't have the time, so I start running around in circles, sort of like a dog, catching up on details. I finish one completely, like the CIA one. Meantime, while I'm waiting to see what happens with it, I'm working on the Robin Williams multiple personality script and thinking about a couple of other things that have been offered to me. Once I get caught up, I usually have two or three projects waiting for me.

FROUG: Do you work with all three of them side by side in your computer?

ROTH: It's all on my desktop computer.

FROUG: Do you just open a screenplay and work on it until you're tired and ready to move on to something else?

ROTH: During the day, every day, I work on my Robin Williams one. That's a first draft, so that requires the most intensive work. At night I will work on something different or I'll work on a rewrite.

FROUG: Does that trouble you, skipping from one screenplay to another?

ROTH: Sometimes I get into a rhythm and I feel badly that I cannot stay in it. But it's not something I do normally.

FROUG: I think you have been in demand since the day you started writing.

ROTH: Well, I don't know about that. I have had a nice career. I have had good luck.

FROUG: It's not luck.

FILMOGRAPHY

1973   *The Nickle Ride*

1979   *The Concorde: Airport '79* (adapted from a novel by Arthur Hailey)

1980   *Suspect*

1981   *Memories of Me* (shared credit)

1982   *Mr. Jones* (shared credit)

1983   *Jane's House*, CBS Movie of the Week

1984   *Forrest Gump* (adapted from the novel by Winston Groom), Academy Award for Best Adapted Screenplay

1985   *The Horse Whisperer* (shared credit, adapted from the novel by Nicholas Evans)

1986   *The Insider* (shared credit), nominated for an Academy Award

Uncredited participating writing on:

1976   *The Drowning Pool*

1979   *The Onion Field*

1981   *Wolfen*

1991   *Rhapsody in August*

1995   *Apollo 13*

"Many people who want to be writers don't really want to be writers.
They want to have been writers."
— James Michener

"Don't give way to violence. The threat or promise or prospect of violence
is eight times as good as violence."
— Nunnally Johnson, *The Screenwriter Looks at the Screenwriter*

"When I was young they called me a liar. Now that I've grown up
they call me a writer."
— Isaac Bashevis Singer, *Written By*, September 1999

Your New Best Friend

G*uilt*

You're facing that blank first page, which you've no doubt written and rewritten dozens of times (sometimes while tossing in bed in the middle of the night). But help is on the way. An invisible friend will save you. He's called Guilt. If you dawdle long enough, waste enough time avoiding writing, your old pal Guilt will show up to remind you that the rent and car payment are due, and that you've promised someone that you'll finish your script by a certain day.

Announce to as many people as possible that you are writing a screenplay that you will finish on a particular date. This helps generate the guilt necessary to force you to work. (Avoiding work is one of the most common characteristics of writers.) Tell your family members and neighbors and maybe a producer or your agent or anyone else who will get on your case if you fail to deliver. However, never tell the *story* that you're writing to anyone. If your friends or family pester you about it, dodge and weave—keep it vague. It must remain your secret. Telling it is the easiest way in the world to transfer your energy away from writing, taking yourself off the hook.

When you are stuck or simply sick of doing what you're doing, often just putting yourself in a potentially humiliating situation will force you to sit down and write. Everybody has pride, and nobody wants to lose it. Countless screenplays have been written with this primary motivation.

Your sense of self-respect and self-worth are on the line right from the get-go. They will nag you, prey on your conscience, corner you so that you have no escape except to write. So to hell with guilt and shame: Write. (Worst case scenario: Your finished screenplay isn't very good.) No matter what, you will at least have delivered on your promise to write—no guilt, no shame there.

You may also push yourself along by entering a screenplay contest. If you enter a contest you always have the pressure of completing your screenplay by the entry date. Some people collapse under the pressure of a deadline, but most writers are energized by a due date.

Write!

If you are determined to become a screenwriter (determination is primary to your success), write until your screenplay is finished; don't stop halfway through it. If it doesn't work, rewrite and rewrite (we all do), and if that doesn't produce a screenplay you're satisfied with, begin another one. As you keep writing and rewriting, you will learn, and you will get better with each script. Or you may decide that this is not the way you would like to make your living. No shame there. Like natural selection, some writers drop by the wayside; others are forced on by sheer grit.

There is no *one* way to write a screenplay; there is only *your* way. Writing backward or forward makes no difference whatsoever, as long as you finish the job. Don't get stopped by the ever-intimidating page one before you get started.

To avoid the awful first-page terrors: As you conceptualize your screenplay and characters, choose a scene that you know you will most likely need in the script—any scene, anyplace in the story—and write it first. It doesn't matter if it turns up on page 16 or 52 or 100 or if, in the final draft, it isn't needed at all. The important thing is that it introduces you to your characters—how they talk, how they behave. Once you've written this scene, you will find you are more comfortable going back to page one, which is no longer as threatening.

As you read in his interview, Nick Kazan began writing his brilliant *Reversal of Fortune* screenplay by writing the last scene first. Why? Because it popped into his mind fully formed. When a good scene just pops into your mind, and it no doubt will, seize the moment. Write it down as quickly as you can; otherwise you might lose it.

Your writer friend

Almost every screenwriter I've ever talked to has a writer friend whose judgment he or she seeks before showing the finished work to anyone else. Mine was the late, great Walter Newman. Once, acting on impulse, I turned in my screenplay to United Artists, as contracted, before showing it to Walter. It cost me dearly. After UA's rejection, Walter gave me the objective critique I had needed earlier but had not sought.

If you don't know anyone in your area who is a screenwriter, make an Internet connection with a fellow aspiring screenwriter. After you connect with a screenwriter, develop the relationship to the point where the two of you discover whether you have similar tastes in movies and whether both of you are on the same learning curve. Continue your discussions. If the relationship deepens and you establish a mutual trust and a working friendship, agree to exchange screenplays for feedback before you submit your script to anyone else. It could be the beginning of a long and fruitful relationship. Having support is an important step in building your career.

A great benefit of this screenwriter-on-screenwriter relationship is that you have someone who will read your work with objectivity and provide you with important feedback. You also have a good source of guilt if you don't deliver. You have now added a real, live, working screenwriter to your old best friend, Guilt. And you are on the path to a new career.

Reality Check

Most of my students were not brilliant screenwriters. Most were average writers. But that's no disgrace. Most of us are average. It has come as no surprise to me that my superstar screenwriting students have gone on to superstar careers. But I have been surprised by how many of my average students have gone on to earn big credits and enjoy big, moneymaking careers. I make no attempt to explain this; I merely report it as fact.

The truth is that there has always been room in the movie business for mediocrity. There just aren't enough geniuses to go around, and there never have been. Go to the movies, watch television, and you will see a lot of mediocrity, including average directors and producers and actors, many of whom enjoy steady work and good livings.

If you can write a solid screenplay with at least a suggestion of originality, you have a shot at making it as a writer. My average students who have gone on to successful careers all had one thing in common: They had to deliver four polished final-draft screenplays to graduate from UCLA's stringent screenwriting program. This suggests to me that if you write four polished final-draft screenplays, you just might get better with each draft. Or maybe you won't become a better writer; maybe you'll become a more persistent writer and create a career through your sheer force of will. It happens.

I know beyond a shadow of a doubt that those "average" former students of mine who now enjoy success were nothing-will-stand-in-my-way writers, driven writers who were determined to make it happen. They did not suddenly turn into geniuses, but they did come up with some unique ideas. The lesson I draw from this is that average may sometimes be good enough, but you will improve your chances for success considerably if you work to make yourself the best writer you can be.

Where It's At

There is nothing new under the sun, yet everything is new under the sun. This is a valuable old adage for screenwriters. Just consider two fairly recent hit movies: *Titanic* and *Shakespeare in Love*.

Titanic was an all-time blockbuster, grossing over a billion dollars. But talk about an old idea! There had already been at least two successful movies about the sinking of that great ocean liner. Many people in Hollywood thought James Cameron was crazy. Why bring out this old turkey again? But Cameron decided to turn this disaster into a love story! Same old material, same old iceberg. All Cameron did was focus our attention on a pair of lovers, using, by the way, almost every cliché in the book.

Shakespeare in Love. What could be more familiar than the works of William Shakespeare? But who knew about his personal life? Who thought to dramatize Shakespeare as a struggling young writer trying to get his career going, facing all the crap every young writer faces, and falling in love while trying to write *Romeo and Juliet*? Screenwriter Marc Norman came up with that very fresh approach. He says that his son actually suggested the idea. (This is most important to note, because all writers take ideas wherever they can find them. It's what we do to survive and thrive.) Sir Tom Stoppard, one of the world's leading playwrights, saw the original qualities of Marc Norman's draft and agreed to do a major rewrite, adding much of the humor that marks his plays. Between the two of them, they came up with an Oscar-winning screenplay—taking the familiar and making it brand new.

History, recent or ancient, is the stuff of great drama, from the very first movie to this week's premiere. Haunt the history section of your local library or bookshop. It's amazing what stories you can unearth in just a few afternoons. Screenwriter William Goldman began his illustrious career writing about two old-West outlaws: Butch Cassidy and the Sundance Kid.

The one thing all great screenwriters I've known or spoken to have in common is that they are avid readers. The single most common advice to beginners that I've heard from these screenwriters is "read." Reading is as important as writing.